Library of
Davidson College

Withdrawn from
Davidson College Library

Arms Control,
the FRG, and the Future
of East-West Relations

About the Book and Editor

The political dimension of arms control has always had special significance for the Federal Republic of Germany, not only because of the issue of a divided Germany and a partitioned Europe but also because of the country's key position in the Western security alliance. In the wake of NATO's recent decision to deploy more nuclear weapons on German soil, and in the absence of progress on arms control, it has become clear that arms control measures and negotiations have assumed an importance far beyond their military-technical components; fundamental questions about the nature of East-West relations and the future shape of the transatlantic alliance and the European political order also have been raised. These essays explore the implications of arms control negotiations for the Federal Republic of Germany and consider why Germany has traditionally found it impossible to divorce considerations of arms control from their larger political context.

Wolfram F. Hanrieder is professor of political science at the University of California, Santa Barbara. He is editor of *Technology, Strategy, and Arms Control* (Westview, 1985) and of *Global Peace and Security: Trends and Challenges* (Westview, 1987).

Published in cooperation with
the Institute on Global Conflict and Cooperation,
University of California, San Diego

Arms Control, the FRG, and the Future of East-West Relations

edited by
Wolfram F. Hanrieder

Westview Press / Boulder and London

Westview Special Studies in National Security and Defense Policy

All rights reserved. No part of this publication may be reproduced or transmitted in any form or by any means, electronic or mechanical, including photocopy, recording, or any information storage and retrieval system, without permission in writing from the publisher.

Copyright © 1987 by Westview Press, Inc.

Published in 1987 in the United States of America by Westview Press, Inc.; Frederick A. Praeger, Publisher; 5500 Central Avenue, Boulder, Colorado 80301

Library of Congress Cataloging-in-Publication Data
Arms control, the FRG, and the future of east-west
  relations.
  (Westview special studies in national security
and defense policy)
  "Published in cooperation with the Institute
on Global Conflict and Cooperation, University of
California, San Diego"—
  Based on papers delivered at a conference held
at the University of California, Santa Barbara,
Nov. 21–22, 1985.
  1. Nuclear arms control—Germany (West)—Congresses.
I. Hanrieder, Wolfram F. II. University of California
Institute on Global Conflict and Cooperation.
III. Series.
JX1974.7.A6745 1987   327.1′74′0943   87-6292
ISBN 0-8133-7353-0

Printed and bound in the United States of America

∞ The paper used in this publication meets the requirements of the American National Standard for Permanence of Paper for Printed Library Materials Z39.48-1984.

10   9   8   7   6   5   4   3   2   1

Contents

Preface ix

1 The Foreign Policy Framework for Arms Control: The Western Alliance and *Ostpolitik, Dietrich Stobbe*   1

2 German and U.S. Perceptions of Arms Control, *Paul E. Zinner*   11

3 The Evolution of West German Public Opinion on Détente Since 1970, *Peter H. Merkl*   29

4 Arms Control in Europe: Prospects and Problems, *Jonathan Dean*   49

5 Extended Deterrence, No First Use, and European Security, *John P. Holdren*   61

6 Star Wars and Arms Control, *Sidney D. Drell*   77

7 Which SDI? *Eckhard Lübkemeier*   85

8 Strategic Defense and the Future of NATO, *Sanford Lakoff*   103

9 SDI: Strategic Disengagement and Independence, *Wolfram F. Hanrieder*   119

List of Acronyms 135
About the Editor and Contributors 137

Preface

The essays collected in this book are based on papers delivered at the University of California, Santa Barbara (UCSB), during a two-day conference, November 21–22, 1985. It is a pleasure to acknowledge the generous support the conference received from the University of California Institute on Global Conflict and Cooperation, the Lounsbery Foundation, and the Volkswagen Foundation.

The spirited discussions that these papers engendered during the conference seemed to indicate that the subject matter—the Federal Republic of Germany (FRG) and arms control—was timely as well as important and that it was charged with far-reaching political implications. Most conference participants were agreed that a consideration of the goals and consequences of arms control requires recognition and acceptance of the reality that arms control inevitably occurs in a political context, a context that either supports or inhibits the prospects for arms control. It is indeed essential to realize that the intentions that drive (or brake) arms control negotiations go beyond the avoidance of war, the stabilization of the military-strategic balance, or the more effective management of crisis situations, and derive their larger meaning from political purposes—global, regional, and domestic. Arms control measures, even as they limit the instruments of war, are the continuation of politics by other means.

For the United States and the Soviet Union, as well as for their respective allies, arms control has always had fundamental implications for the nature of East-West relations, for the management of their security alliances, and hence for the shape of the global and European political order. The limits that define mutually acceptable arms control arrangements have always been at the same time the limits that define political accommodation. When these limits have proven insufficiently flexible, neither political purpose nor arms control could be realized.

The political dimensions of arms control have always had a special significance for the Federal Republic of Germany. Because of Germany's history, even the thought of a German finger on the nuclear trigger casts a shadow; and even the Germans' association with conventional arms remains vaguely threatening, although they themselves feel vaguely insecure. Although more than four decades have passed since most of Europe suffered at the hands of German military might, European sensitivities (both in the West and in the East) have remained sharp; and many Germans themselves demonstrate a commendable moral sensibility in their often uneasy relationship with military matters, conventional or nuclear.

The history of West German attitudes toward arms control is complex, as are the calculations, feelings, and aspirations that go into the Germans' reactions to the arms control issues of the 1980s. For historical, moral, psychological, and ultimately political reasons, German diplomacy in the 1950s and 1960s would have been more effective if the Bonn government had managed to develop a more constructive attitude toward arms control. But powerful obstacles stood in the way. Above all, the tortuous response of successive German governments to the East-West arms control proposals of the 1950s and 1960s—disengagement plans, the test ban treaty, the nonproliferation treaty—stemmed from misgivings over their repercussions on the issue of Germany's division and from the attempt, by and large unsuccessful, to exert a greater influence in the management of the transatlantic security pact and in its institutional arrangements in the North Atlantic Treaty Organization (NATO). It wasn't until the 1970s, when Bonn's *Ostpolitik* became an essential part of East-West détente—a process that was itself sustained by partial agreements on arms control and by the mutual readiness to legitimize the European status quo—that the government of the FRG could approach arms control with a more constructive and less hesitant attitude.

In the 1980s, arms control was deprived of the supportive political base that the mutual East-West interest in solidifying the European status quo had provided in the early and mid-1970s and there was no easy or obvious answer to the question of which East-West issue of the 1980s would lend itself to playing a similar role. In the wake of NATO's decision to deploy more nuclear weapons on German soil, and in the absence of progress on arms control, the Germans arrived at the uneasy realization that the increased nuclear saturation of both German states tied them even closer to their superpower protectors and their respective views of the East-West contest; underlined the division of Europe and of Germany; and narrowed the range of East-West diplomacy. In the early and mid-1980s it became, once again, irrefutably clear that arms control measures, important as they may be in their own right, took on a meaning that went far beyond their military-technical import and raised fundamental questions about the nature of East-West relations and the future shape of the transatlantic alliance and the European political order. These are some of the issues that the essays collected here explore.

Wolfram F. Hanrieder
Santa Barbara, California

1

The Foreign Policy Framework for Arms Control: The Western Alliance and *Ostpolitik*

Dietrich Stobbe

Arms Control and Foreign Policy

Arms control and disarmament are today among the most important issues facing the nations involved in the East-West conflict. These issues cannot be considered in isolation from the overall relations between East and West because progress on arms control is achievable only if the political climate between the two alliances permits such progress. As a result, the foreign policy environment plays a decisive role in successes or failures of arms control policy.

What applies to all the nations involved in the East-West conflict applies particularly to divided Germany, making disarmament and arms control a focal point of German political endeavors. The government of the Federal Republic of Germany (FRG) has voluntarily renounced control over nuclear, biological, and chemical weapons, thus making a major contribution of its own toward arms control and disarmament. Yet, both the FRG and the German Democratic Republic (GDR) are faced with the disturbing fact that large quantities of such weapons are stockpiled on their territories as a result of the confrontation between the systems of East and West, a confrontation that has divided Europe and has drawn the sharpest dividing line through Germany. A basic fact of international relations determines the guidelines for the Federal Republic in the area of arms control: as much defense as necessary, as much arms control and disarmament as possible.

The governments of the Federal Republic of Germany and the German Democratic Republic cannot discuss issues of arms control within a narrow national framework; their freedom to maneuver is limited. In the economic field and in the area of conventional weapons, each German state has become the most important alliance partner of its respective leading power—an irony when one considers that World War II, begun by Germany, gave rise to two world powers that today ensure the balance on the European continent. The fact that both German states are of crucial importance to the two alliances makes their arms control policies an international issue of great significance. The reverse is also true: Arms control or armament decisions made by other member states of the alliances—in particular, of course, the United States and the USSR—almost always have a major, direct impact on the situation in Germany. (The extensive debate and final decision on the intermediate-range missiles is a good example.)

Acceptance of military parity between the United States and the Soviet Union and of the territorial status quo in Europe, the Helsinki process, and the declared readiness of both superpowers for mutual restraint in the Third World—these were the parameters for détente in the 1970s. Yet it is worth noting that arms control and disarmament were not prominently featured in this list. Although arms control and disarmament were considered to be important political aims, many assumed that the higher level of confidence in East-West relations generated by détente would automatically lead to progress in achieving these aims. The disappointment when these results failed to materialize overshadows political discussions of arms control.

We Social Democrats in the Federal Republic therefore believe that a second phase of détente can be constructively initiated only if the element of "common security," or of "mutual assured security," is added to the factors that have been applicable so far. This concept is called "security partnership between East and West." The formula set forth in the Harmel Report of 1967, according to which security is a product of defense plus détente, must be extended; the excessive level of armaments that distinguishes current East-West relations has created a situation in which those on each side must begin to recognize that in seeking to enhance their own security, they must also be mindful of the security interests of the other side. Precisely because progress on arms control, important as it is in itself, is dependent on other issues, the two superpowers need to make progress toward cooperation regarding trouble spots in the Third World. If a second phase of détente is to take effect, the term "mutual restraint" in the 1972 Declaration of Principles between the two superpowers needs to be more clearly defined. Faith in détente in the United States was shattered primarily because Soviet conduct in some areas of the Third World was perceived as expansionistic, as incompatible with the principles agreed upon by the two superpowers. This basic factor of foreign policy has been, and continues to be, crucial in handling the East-West conflict, and it has direct repercussions for the issues of arms control and disarmament in the Federal Republic.

Germany's Place on the World Stage in the 1980s: An International Debate

Germany's future is inextricably linked to relations between the United States and the Soviet Union. During the cold war, German reunification was a central issue in the East-West conflict; during the period of détente, a *modus vivendi* between the Federal Republic of Germany and the German Democratic Republic was reached. This *modus vivendi* provided the basic premise for the FRG's *Ostpolitik*. During the last few years, however, relations between the United States and the Soviet Union again deteriorated and reached their lowest point in a long time. The atmosphere and issues that prevailed in Europe in the 1950s and the 1960s have apparently revisted us. Divided Germany is again a controversial issue that is the subject of intense discussion in the capitals of both Western and Eastern Europe.

Recent developments at both ends of our domestic political spectrum have fueled the international controversy, showing up also certain illusions on the Left as well as on the Right. The question of Germany's geographical borders has been revived by the political Right in the FRG. Members of the federal government and other high-ranking politicians of the ruling coalition have asserted the continuing existence of the German Reich within the borders of 1937. Such claims naturally provoke strong reactions in Eastern Europe, particularly in Poland. Moreover, some argue that German reunification is a necessary precondition for a "European peace order." These viewpoints endanger the modicum of practical cooperation with the GDR that has been achieved with so much difficulty.

On the other hand, new neutralist tendencies in the FRG, calling for the withdrawal of the FRG and the GDR from the existing military alliances, have generated other concerns. Anxiety that the Germans might take a neutralist stand has an irritating effect on international politics, comparable to that produced by the reunification issue. Illusory talk of reunification and border revision, on the one hand, and unrealistic demands for neutrality, on the other, are dangerous developments that must be opposed.

A thorough analysis of the political process in the FRG reveals that the vast majority of Germans reject both of these political stances. Germans understand that successful East-West cooperation has made a *modus vivendi* possible and has provided a realistic framework for a tolerable, and perhaps eventually even a "good," relationship between the two German states. It is evident that the present international circumstances permit only small and laborious steps. Working toward East-West understanding has thus developed into a kind of German national obligation. It is our special contribution to peace—to maintain the era of *modus vivendi* and rule out radical solutions, such as immediate reunification or neutrality. This is the most fundamental and most challenging task for the Federal Republic; the state's room to maneuver and the possibilities for arms control are closely linked to this task.

Policymaking in the Federal Republic of Germany Since 1945

Three major factors of the FRG's policies continue to determine the West German role in the Western alliance and on the world stage. The first is our commitment to democratic values. In contrast to the United States, Germany failed to bring about a successful democratic revolution. Not until after 1945 was democracy firmly established in Germany, and then only in the FRG. But in the FRG the commitment to democracy has grown and its enduring nature has revealed itself in recent years.

The second factor is the goal of German unity. Germans in East and West bear heavy guilt for having begun a war of aggression that resulted in the deaths of 60 million people: The only period of German national unity within the German Reich—the seventy-four years from 1871 to 1945—closed with a balance sheet of horror, thus discrediting the idea of German unity in the eyes of other nations. Yet the human, economic, and political burden of the division is too immense for the Germans to ignore; every German government must confront the question of unity.

The third factor of the FRG's policies has been Western integration. The history of the postwar period has established the Federal Republic as an integral part of the West. Integration in the West has been the essential precondition for the FRG's *Ostpolitik* rather than an alternative to it. Membership in the Western alliance limits the scope and maneuverability of any "national" policy that the Federal Republic could pursue.

Together these three elements—the commitment to democracy, the goal of German unity, and integration in the Western alliance—exert a decisive influence on the policy of successive West German governments, resulting in clear political priorities.

For the FRG, peace is the essential precondition for any freedom of action. There is a fundamental consensus and deep conviction in Germany that war must never again start from German soil. A war waged with today's high technology weapons would, in all likelihood, destroy the countries of Central Europe. The awareness that Germans must either get along with one another or die with one another determines political attitudes in both German states.

West German policy therefore subordinates reunification to peace. Although the FRG's constitution, the Basic Law, obliges Germans to seek unity, a sense of reality and historical responsibility prevails. It is thus more important to secure our own freedom within the FRG and to bring about more freedom for the East Germans than to overemphasize the theme of national unity to the point at which the GDR might reject negotiation and rule out any change or the possibility of gradual transition. This priority is advisable because the GDR cannot accept the concept of reunification without questioning its own existence as the other German state—hence the distinction that is seen in the Federal Republic's constitution, which speaks of national unity not of reunification. For the majority of Germans, the goal of reestablishing a large German state, composed of the remaining elements of the defeated German Reich, has become increasingly unrealistic. But the goal of greater German cooperation, as an element of a process in the course of which the nations of Europe grow closer together, has met with a favorable response. In other words, a European cooperative framework might serve to lessen the antagonisms between the two systems.

The Power Structure in Eastern Europe: Is Change Possible?

Through the German Democratic Republic, the Soviet Union defends the gains it made as a result of World War II. The Soviet Union became a world power by extending its political sphere to the River Elbe, and nothing suggests that its government would be willing to relinquish its dominance over the Eastern European states in the realms of foreign policy, security, and ideology. Obviously, the Soviet Union needs a predictable and stable GDR to help secure its control over Eastern and Central Europe.

Nevertheless there have been significant changes in the power structures within the Warsaw Pact. (The GDR's internal and external position under Erich Honecker is, for example, different from that under Walter Ulbricht.) These changes can partly be attributed to the consequences of détente. The striving of the GDR and the other East European nations for greater external and internal independence from the Soviet Union cannot be overlooked. These aspirations have been, and will undoubtedly remain, a vital and constructive part of the process of any successful East-West cooperation.

Two Germanys Within Separate Alliances: Crucial Contributors to Stability

The two German states can play a major role in potential East-West cooperation. In terms of conventional military strength and economic power they have become the strongest partners for their respective superpower allies. This gives the two German states considerable influence and makes them indispensable allies. The alliance structures that have developed over three decades in both East and West could not be changed without enormous repercussions, potentially jeopardizing regional stability. Consequently, the two German states can only pursue policies which promote East-West cooperation within their respective alliances and through these alliances. Any withdrawal from the alliances would reduce German influence and diminish the chances of safeguarding peace.

Alliance Cohesion and the Urgency of Arms Control

How can the task of preserving the situation described above retain sufficient appeal for future generations of Germans? The pressures of this situation were especially evident in the intermediate-range nuclear force (INF) debate. The Federal Republic did what was necessary to preserve the unity of the alliance but the debate revealed new strains and domestic policy limits to the Federal Republic's ability to persevere. Bitter disappointment at the failure to achieve meaningful reconciliation of East-West interests in the field of intermediate-range nuclear weapons has alienated many people from the defense and détente consensus that NATO enjoyed for many years.

In the German view, the dialogue on arms control and disarmament forms the vital core of effective superpower cooperation, and because this dialogue has stagnated over the years in such a discouraging manner, many West Germans now desire to exert greater influence on the arms control efforts. This is true certainly for those people who still preserve trust in the ability of the U.S. and the USSR to maintain peace so far. Undoubtedly some German citizens have abandoned that hope, seeking solutions for Europe independent of or even against the superpowers.

West German Foreign Policy Options: National, European, or Atlantic-Global?

Three foreign policy options confront West Germany. Though not all of them may be viable, these options avoid extremes and deserve serious and careful analysis.

1. *National*. The German-German community of responsibility has played an important role in past years. It is based on the idea that the two German states have to make a special contribution to keeping détente in Europe alive. Even after the change in the Bonn government—with the shift from the social-liberal to the conservative-liberal coalition—considerable (although not sufficient) continuity has been practiced in the name of this concept. Both German states have been able to make constructive contributions aimed at keeping the East-West conflict in Europe under control. Pursuant to a provision in the Basic Treaty, both sides have to some extent even been able to take initiatives for arms control and disarmament. One such initiative, for example, is the proposal made in 1985 for a chemical weapons–free zone in Central Europe drawn up jointly by the Social Democratic Party (SPD) and the East German Socialist Unity Party (SED).

However, the German community of responsibility is an inappropriate instrument when it is used to propagate a kind of intra-German détente. The state of relations between the United States and the Soviet Union has a greater impact on the relations between the two German states than on relations between any other nations in Europe. The limits to their freedom of action, which the two German states cannot overcome by themselves, have become clearly apparent. The concept is not able to fulfill either German national or German neutralist dreams. However, as a building block for East-West cooperation, which is supported by all European states, the German-German community of responsibility is indispensable.

2. *European*. The ambitious concept of a re-Europeanization of Europe is based on the idea of the Europe of the fatherlands, both on this side of the political dividing line and beyond it. The desire of the European nations to base their relations on a continuous exchange with each other proved to be a strong force also in the light of the tough confrontation between the two superpowers in the last few years. This concept seeks unity in diversity and considers it possible for the Eastern European communist systems gradually to develop into liberal, socialist societies. As a means of achieving this goal it offers a kind of East-West cooperation among the European nations, organized alongside the two superpowers. Many Europeans perceive the superpowers as prisoners of their global rivalry, tied down by acute conflicts in other parts of the world. According to this concept, the European nations should, in a gradual process, increasingly dissociate themselves from the dominance of the superpowers and shape a process of East-West cooperation in Europe that becomes increasingly independent of the deadly duel being fought by the two superpowers.

However, the dream of an autonomous European détente is ahistoric; time and again, it clashes with reality, namely with the fact that the U.S. and USSR control the European center and guarantee the new balance on the European continent. The concept of re-Europeanization of Europe is defective in that it does not adequately take into account the two superpowers' play in Europe.

3. *Atlantic-Global.* The third option is directed at producing changes in the transatlantic alliance. It is being pursued with a view toward strengthening the European pillar of NATO. Greater European self-assertion or, to be more precise, greater self-assertion of the Western European members of NATO, is intended to make it possible to counter unilateralist tendencies in U.S. policymaking vis-à-vis the Eastern alliance. For this concept to become reality, the French government will have to revise its political relationship with NATO by abandoning its narrow definition of national defense and becoming more responsive to the idea of European defense. For its part, the Federal Republic will be able to exert influence only if it remains a member of the Western alliance and becomes the champion of strong European self-assertion among its Western European members. Only in this way can the Federal Republic of Germany remain equally committed to Western integration and to *Ostpolitik*. The FRG's task therefore consists in helping ensure that the nations of Western Europe organize themselves and join forces in the foreign and defense policy field in such a way that their influence on Western policies toward the Eastern alliance is strengthened. Seen in this light, this third option too aims to make a contribution to regulating the East-West conflict.

Conclusion

The Federal Republic of Germany has a crucial interest in arms control and disarmament. However, it cannot go it alone in this field—all solutions must be devised in an international framework. To the West, the Federal Republic is integrated in an alliance that is committed to the defense and development of the basic freedoms, and the decision in favor of these values is irreversible. By means of *Ostpolitik*, the Federal Republic is pursuing its fundamental interest in mitigating the consequences of the division of the German nation. In so doing, it is at the same time serving the cause of freedom and peace. The Federal Republic does not face an either/or decision between Western integration and *Ostpolitik*, but it needs, time and again, to recombine these different tasks and place them on a sound international basis. The Western alliance should always be aware of and respect the peculiarity of the German situation because the alliance can only be as good as the sum total of the interests of all of its members.

For the Federal Republic's foreign policy, arms control and disarmament raise extraordinarily complex issues. The efforts to achieve arms control will be successful if the leading Western power, the United States, and the leading Eastern power, the Soviet Union, acknowledge that security in the nuclear world depends more on political efforts to reduce tension than on weapons themselves.

2

German and U.S. Perceptions of Arms Control

Paul E. Zinner

Historical Background

The beginnings of the East-West arms control process may be traced to the administration of President John F. Kennedy in the early 1960s. The road ahead would be tortuous. Ironically, what Kennedy initiated actually came to fruition under the presidency of his political arch rival, Richard M. Nixon. Throughout the 1960s, however, despite major setbacks—such as the Berlin Wall (1961); the Cuban Missile Crisis (1962); the massive expansion of the Vietnam War (1965); the Six-Day War in the Middle East (1967); and, finally, the Warsaw Pact (WP) invasion of Czechoslovakia (1968)—recurring efforts as well as a modicum of progress were made by the United States and the Soviet Union to explore the possibility of bilateral negotiations, specifically concerning the control of nuclear arms. In early 1969, shortly after his inauguration, President Nixon proclaimed a formal shift in U.S. foreign policy toward the USSR, from confrontation to negotiation. The Soviet Union responded in kind.

In Europe, a parallel trend was evolving. France, which withdrew its military forces from the integrated military command structure of NATO in 1966, followed up with a bid to the Soviet Union for improved relations. Both military blocs—NATO and the Warsaw Pact—gave indications that they sought a relaxation of tensions. Thus, the Warsaw Pact at a meeting in Bucharest (1966) issued a declaration that proposed the convening of a Conference on Security and Cooperation in Europe (CSCE). The proposal was reiterated at a WP meeting in Budapest in 1969. NATO, in turn, at its ministerial meeting in December 1967, adopted a study report prepared under the leadership of Pierre Harmel (the Belgian foreign minister) that called for the development of stable political relations in Europe as the second major function of the alliance, equal in importance to its primary function of providing for the deterrent and defense capability of the West.

Meanwhile, the contours of an arms reduction program in Europe also emerged. As early as 1959, Helmut Schmidt, a Bundestag deputy of the Social Democratic Party (SPD), outlined a mutual and balanced force reduction (MBFR) project affecting conventional forces in Central Europe. (It might be noted in passing that he envisaged a residual ceiling, after reductions, of 300,000 troops for the West and 400,000 troops for the East.) Schmidt gave further substance to this project at the Dortmund Congress of the SPD in June 1966. Two years later in 1968, NATO foreign ministers evolved an MBFR concept at their meeting in Reykjavik, Iceland. This was followed up in December 1969 with a charge to the standing NATO council to elaborate a model for balanced troop reductions in Europe. In May 1970, the NATO Ministerial Council adopted a second MBFR declaration, this time as a specific negotiating offer to the East.

Clearly, the Federal Republic of Germany had a major stake in these developments and was significantly affected by them. Attitudes toward the prospect of détente were ambivalent, and they changed throughout the 1960s. In the early 1960s, the government of Konrad Adenauer strongly opposed a possible Soviet-U.S. rapprochement because it was concerned that the superpowers might reach an accommodation that would be detrimental to the interests of the FRG and in conflict with its policy of isolating the GDR and its goal of German reunification. In the middle and late 1960s, West German views concerning relations with the East became more differentiated. Ultimately, with the creation of a social-liberal coalition following Parliamentary elections in 1969, a policy of reconciliation with the East was adopted. The new *Ostpolitik* was predicated on the acceptance of the post-war territorial status quo, which entailed recognition of the existence of the GDR.

Initiatives that France and the United States had taken in regulating their relations with the Soviet Union were an important factor in inducing the West German government to seek a normalization of relations with the Soviet Union and its East European allies (especially Poland and the GDR) in order to avoid diplomatic and political isolation in Europe. FRG policymakers must also have been influenced by perceived changes in the strategic balance between the United States and the USSR.[1] These changes, which tended to erode the credibility of U.S. strategic arms as a reliable shield for NATO, found expression in a shift from "massive retaliation" to "flexible response" as a more suitable doctrine, giving the alliance more articulated options for deterring and, if need be, responding to WP aggression. The new doctrine was adopted by NATO in 1967, after seven years of discussion.

In the early 1970s, the structure of détente was hammered into place.

- In 1970, the United States and the USSR began talks to limit their strategic arms—the Strategic Arms Limitation Talks (SALT). These negotiations culminated in the signing of an agreement (SALT I) in 1972 at the first Moscow summit between President Nixon and General Secretary Leonid Brezhnev. In Europe, preliminary negotiations about security and cooperation began in November 1972 in Helsinki, and preparatory MBFR talks got underway in Vienna in January 1973.
- The Four Powers (the United States, the United Kingdom, France, and the USSR) reached agreement about the status of Berlin in September 1971. The agreement entered into force in June 1972.
- The FRG, for its part, signed a treaty with the USSR in August 1970. This was followed by a treaty in December 1970 with the People's Republic of Poland, concerning the basis for normalizing their mutual relations, and a treaty in December 1972 on the basis of relations (*Grundlagenvertrag*) with the German Democratic Republic.

FRG Perceptions of Arms Control Under Détente

Arms control and disarmament negotiations were an integral part of détente in Europe and of a relaxation of tensions between the United States and the Soviet Union. Two separate negotiations were conducted, one in which the superpowers were involved along with some members of their respective alliance systems (MBFR), and another that was of a bilateral nature (SALT). Negotiations in Europe in which the two alliances were involved concerned conventional force reductions and affected only the regional or theater balance of these forces. Direct Soviet-U.S. negotiations about strategic arms, of course, affected the security of the two superpowers, but they also affected the security of the European member states of NATO. This was bound to cause apprehension, especially in the FRG, which is a frontier state directly exposed to WP aggression and thus commensurately more dependent on U.S. military protection.

SALT talks and agreements had a potentially disruptive effect on relations between the United States and the Federal Republic of Germany. On the one hand, they were viewed with approval in the FRG as a welcome expression of East-West accommodation; on the other hand, they aroused suspicions in the FRG as a possible source of the country's diminished security. In general, SALT I was regarded by West Germans as confirmation of the mutual paralysis of the strategic arms of the two superpowers. Under these conditions, the value of U.S. strategic arms was severely restricted—if not nullified—as a deterrent to and defense against WP aggression. The United States would be putting its own territorial security at risk if it attempted to use them in a regional, European setting. The specter of decoupling European security from that of the United States began to haunt the West Germans. Without an effective nuclear shield, the disparity between WP and NATO conventional forces became more threatening.

Whether a better balance could be established through MBFR was questionable. Why would the Soviet Union give up at the negotiating table an advantage it had in the field? Moreover, some aspects of an MBFR agreement, as formulated by the Soviet Union, seemed designed primarily to constrain the FRG and therefore were unacceptable to it. For example, the setting of national instead of collective alliance ceilings for the residual troop strength of participating countries after reduction would establish an absolute limit for the Federal Republic's entire military (because all of the FRG's territory was in the reduction area). The military of other major powers (USSR, United States, and United Kingdom) would be affected only to the extent to which they had troops in the reduction area. France and Italy would remain altogether unaffected: the first, because it did not participate in the talks; the second, because it was an associated rather than a direct participant and its territory did not fall within the reduction zone. Not only did the government of the FRG feel discriminated against in comparison to those of other major powers, it felt that the establishment of an absolute ceiling for its military through international agreement would be an encroachment on its sovereignty.[2]

Although the FRG had a substantial interest in lowering the troop strength of opposing forces concentrated on its Eastern border, the policy it pursued in the Vienna talks seemed ambiguous, if not obstructionist. In the latter part of the 1970s, this became a contentious issue between the SPD and its coalition partner, the liberal Free Democratic Party (FDP). Herbert Wehner (the redoubtable floor leader of the SPD in the Bundestag) publicly accused Hans-Dietrich Genscher (the FDP foreign minister, whose jurisdiction encompassed arms control matters) of dragging his feet in the Vienna talks.[3] Genscher rejected the charges, and the FRG's posture in Vienna did not change. When Chancellor Schmidt suggested the introduction of a 50 percent formula (no country on either side should have a greater share than 50 percent of the total forces of the alliance to which it belonged), Genscher simply ignored the matter.[4] The FRG never introduced a proposal to this effect in Vienna. Internal squabbling over MBFR, however, had an insignificant impact in comparison with growing apprehensions about the implications of the SALT process.

Differentiation Between U.S. and FRG Perceptions

Although strongly favoring arms control and disarmament negotiations as confidence-building measures that help to create a benign climate for nurturing détente, the government of the FRG (in the second half of the 1970s) became increasingly concerned about the widening gap between NATO's deterrent and defense capabilities and the offensive capacities of the WP. The main source of these concerns was the realization that the Soviet Union had developed a new type of medium-range nuclear system (the SS-20, a mobile, reloadable missile with three warheads). The SS-20, together with the Backfire bomber, represented a serious threat to the security of Western Europe that NATO could not counter. The integrity of the doctrine of "flexible response" was in jeopardy. But because these Soviet systems had a limited range, they were no threat to the continental United States. For want of a better term, they were referred to as "grey zone" systems. Their range differentiated them from both short-range battlefield and long-range strategic systems, and they were not encompassed in either one of the ongoing arms control negotiations—MBFR or SALT.

Chancellor Schmidt sought to alert the administration of President Jimmy Carter about the dangers he perceived in this development. He requested clarification about U.S. arms control policy in the light of this new threat and pressed the U.S. administration to include consideration of these systems in the SALT II agenda.[5] His interventions in Washington were not well received; they were resented there and repulsed as gratuitous meddling in a sphere of responsibility belonging exclusively to the United States.

Personal incompatibility between Chancellor Schmidt and Zbigniew Brzezinski (President Carter's national security advisor) compounded the problem of reaching mutually satisfactory understanding about complicated and difficult objective issues that confronted the Federal Republic of Germany and the United States.[6] Communications between them were strained; West Germans felt that they were not consulted nor even adequately informed about matters that had a vital impact on their security. In exasperation, Chancellor Schmidt aired his apprehensions in a public forum in the compass of the Alastair Buchan Memorial Lecture, which he delivered in October 1977 at the International Institute of Strategic Studies in London. It is generally believed that this address gave impetus to the process that ultimately resulted in the stationing of U.S. intermediate-range nuclear systems in Europe. Because of other intervening circumstances that could not have been anticipated, the unleashing of a chain of developments attributed to Chancellor Schmidt led to a highly divisive experience for NATO and contributed to a serious aggravation of East-West relations in Europe.

The chancellor's comments deserve to be quoted extensively and to be read with close attention. (For the sake of greater clarity, I took the liberty of lifting the first passage I quote from the sequence in which it appears in the chancellor's text. Emphasis added.)

> When the SALT negotiations opened we Europeans did not have a clear enough view of the close connection between parity of strategic nuclear weapons, on the one hand, and *tactical nuclear* and conventional weapons on the other, or if we did, we did not articulate it clearly enough. Today we need to recognize clearly the connection between SALT and MBFR and to draw the necessary practical conclusions.[7]

The chancellor's admission that Europeans initially underestimated the close connection between parity of weapons systems on all levels of the escalatory spectrum is as startling as it is candid. It is also interesting that he apparently designates intermediate-range, Eurostrategic systems as tactical nuclear weapons.

The remaining passages of his address are quoted here in their original sequence.

> We should recognize that—paradoxical as it may sound—there is a closer proximity between a hazardous arms race, on the one hand, and a successful control of arms, on the other, than ever before. There is only a narrow divide between the hope for peace and the danger of war.
>
> . . . changed strategic conditions confront us with new problems. SALT codifies the nuclear strategic balance between the Soviet Union and the United States. To put it another way: SALT neutralizes their strategic nuclear capabilities. In Europe this magnifies the significance of the disparities between East and West *in nuclear tactical* and conventional weapons. . . .
>
> No one can deny that the principle of parity is a sensible one. However, its fulfilment must be the aim of all arms-limitation and arms-control negotiations and it must apply *to all categories of weapons*. Neither side can agree to diminish its security unilaterally.
>
> It is of vital interest to us all that the negotiations between the two superpowers on the limitation and reduction of nuclear strategic weapons should continue and lead to a lasting agreement. The nuclear powers have a special, an overwhelming responsibility in this field. On the other hand, we in Europe must be particularly careful to ensure that these negotiations do not neglect the components of NATO's deterrence strategy.

We are all faced with the dilemma of having to meet the moral and political demand for arms limitation while at the same time maintaining a fully effective deterrent to war. We are not unaware that both the United States and the Soviet Union must be anxious to remove threatening strategic developments from their relationship. But strategic arms limitations confined to the United States and the Soviet Union will inevitably impair the security of the West European members of the (Western) Alliance vis-à-vis Soviet military superiority in Europe if we do not succeed in removing the disparities of military power in Europe parallel to the SALT negotiations. So long as this is not the case *we must maintain the balance of the full range of deterrence strategy.* The Alliance must, therefore, be ready *to make available the means to support its present strategy*, which is still the right one, and to prevent any developments that could undermine the basis of this strategy. . . .

[The passage quoted out of sequence fits here.]

. . . in theory, [there are] two possible ways of establishing a conventional balance with the Warsaw Pact states. One would be for the Western Alliance to undertake a massive buildup of forces and weapons systems; the other for both NATO and the Warsaw Pact to reduce their force strength and achieve an overall balance at a lower level. I prefer the latter.

Two things stand out in the chancellor's trenchant analysis. First, he makes no specific reference to actual tactical nuclear weapons systems. Second, he leaves room for interpreting his preferences for the solution of the problems that he identifies. He states that in regard to establishing a conventional balance in Europe, he prefers force reductions to a massive buildup of forces and weapons systems. However, he also states that so long as disparities of military power in Europe—which by his own definition include tactical nuclear and conventional weapons—are not removed parallel to the SALT negotiations, a balance across the full range of deterrence strategy must be maintained. This implies that to offset Soviet superiority in both tactical nuclear and conventional weapons, appropriate nuclear systems would have to be placed at NATO's disposal and its conventional forces would have to be built up. The ambiguities in Chancellor Schmidt's statement may account for differing interpretations of his intent. Some felt he clearly opted for arms control. Others thought he pleaded for beefed-up NATO deterrence and defense capability in order to restore the integrity of the doctrine of "flexible response."

The U.S. government chose the latter interpretation and responded with an offer to counter the new Soviet threat potential with the deployment of U.S. nuclear weapons in Europe (Pershing II missiles [PIIs] and ground-launched cruise missiles [GLCMs]). Chancellor Schmidt professed to have been "relatively surprised" when President Carter broached this subject at an informal meeting of four heads of state and government in Guadeloupe early in 1979.[8] The three European leaders who were present—French President Giscard d'Estaing, British Prime Minister James Callaghan, and Chancellor Schmidt—recommended that negotiations with the Soviet Union should precede deployment, but that it should be understood that deployment would take place if no satisfactory agreement were reached on the reduction or elimination of the Soviet weapons in question. The leaders felt that the Soviet government would negotiate seriously only if it knew that the alternative to negotiations was the stationing of U.S. weapons in Europe.

For the remainder of 1979—in fact for President Carter's entire term—relations between the Federal Republic and the United States reflected discord over arms control and related matters that affected détente in Europe in general.

Conclusion of the SALT II Agreement

The signing of SALT II by President Carter and General Secretary Brezhnev in Vienna in June 1979 was greeted with muted enthusiasm in the FRG. Approval was conditioned by expectations of rapid ratification by the U.S. Senate and a quick transition to SALT III negotiations in which European security concerns would be duly attended to. Some Germans were bitter about SALT II. Walther Stützle (the head of the planning staff in the Defense Ministry until October 1982, when the social-liberal coalition was replaced by a conservative-liberal government) subsequently wrote that in SALT II "the United States for the first time since the Second World War confirmed, by presidential signature, that the Soviet Union could threaten with certain weapons systems only Western Europe, but not the United States."[9] In other words, the concept of indivisible alliance security was shattered. What Stützle and others attacked was, of course, not the principle of arms negotiations reflected in SALT II, but what they perceived to be the objectives that the United States had pursued in these negotiations, to the detriment of its West European alliance partners. The security of Western Europe was decoupled from that of the United States.

The NATO Double-track Decision

In the second half of 1979, NATO moved toward the adoption of its double-track decision in an atmosphere of rapidly deepening international crisis. This decision called for negotiations about Soviet middle-range nuclear systems threatening Europe and deployment of U.S. systems, if these negotiations failed. The U.S. government was chafing under the indignities it had recently suffered in Iran, where its embassy was occupied by rebellious students and the entire embassy staff was taken hostage. The Carter administration was in no mood to trifle with the Soviet Union, which gave unmistakable evidence of wanting to head off the double-track decision. Initiatives to this effect by Soviet General Secretary Brezhnev were summarily rejected in Washington as attempts to interfere in the affairs of the Western alliance. Suspicions also spread about Chancellor Schmidt's steadfastness.[10] Nevertheless, at an SPD Congress in West Berlin only a few days before the NATO ministerial meeting, Schmidt marshalled substantial support for the double-track decision, despite fairly widespread opposition to it within the party.

The adoption of the double-track decision on December 12, 1979, did not allay misgivings in the FRG that the U.S. government had a hidden agenda favoring deployment of nuclear missiles in Europe. Germans, of course, also had a hidden agenda that favored negotiations, hoping that these would help to stave off deployment. In other words, the double-track decision was perceived in the FRG essentially as a means of furthering arms control in Europe and thus, in the broader context, of promoting détente. But the possibility that the implementation of the double-track decision—through the stationing of U.S. nuclear missiles—could in fact worsen East-West relations (while, of course, at the same time reflecting a worsening of these relations) and supply the United States with an instrument for establishing the basis of conducting limited war in Europe struck fear into the hearts of many Germans.

The Aftermath of the USSR Invasion of Afghanistan

In the circumstances that ensued—namely, the Soviet invasion of Afghanistan at the end of December 1979 and the frenzied U.S. response to it—hopes for arms control negotiations under the aegis of the NATO double-track decisions dwindled. The superpowers were in sharp conflict, and the breakdown of superpower détente was viewed with alarm in the FRG. Although Soviet aggression was assessed there as a serious transgression of the norms of international behavior, the sanctions invoked by the United States against the USSR were also criticized. Still, the FRG supported some of them (such as the ban on participating in the Moscow Olympic Games in the summer of 1980), albeit reluctantly.

Although it was stunned by President Carter's withdrawal of SALT II from Senate consideration, the FRG government was at pains to bring the superpowers to the negotiating table to discuss medium-range missiles in Europe. To this end, Chancellor Schmidt journeyed to Moscow at the end of June.[11] His effort was successful: The Soviet leaders found the occasion propitious to agree to negotiations under certain conditions, thus saving face by making it appear that by relenting from their opposition to negotiations, they were responding to the German chancellor's pleas. Schmidt's Moscow journey was celebrated as a triumph in Bonn, while in Washington it was viewed with skepticism.[12] Nevertheless, preliminary talks about medium-range nuclear force reductions (officially designated as long-range theater nuclear force, of LRTNF, a designation that changed to intermediate-range nuclear force, or INF, under President Reagan) opened in Geneva in October. The talks were suspended before the U.S. presidential elections and were not reconvened until thirteen months later, on November 30, 1981.

Bonn and the Reagan Administration

Under the presidency of Ronald Reagan, a major reassessment (and temporary suspension) of the arms control process took place. The new administration gave primacy to an arms buildup instead. Basic assumptions underlying the arms control process as an integral part of Western security policy toward the East (deterrence *and* arms control) were challenged and revised. A dichotomy was presumed to exist between security (*Sicherheit*) and détente (*Entspannung*), and a choice had to be made for one or the other.

The pragmatic-diplomatic action model that had informed East-West relations during the preceding decade (despite misunderstandings based on divergent perceptions of problems and their appropriate solution) gave way to a geopolitically and ideologically motivated approach. Global rivalry with the USSR became the dominant conflict image.[13]

By contrast, the FRG's faith in arms control as an integral and indispensable part of the détente process was undaunted, although arms control efforts had so far produced disappointing results. They had not diminished distrust, especially between the United States and the USSR, and they had failed miserably as a confidence-building measure.

Resurgent superpower confrontation did not accord with the FRG's perception of its security interests. The fact that negotiations about medium-range nuclear weapons remained in abeyance for a second year after the adoption of the NATO double-track decision caused unrest among the German public, especially because the talks were time limited: If they produced no results by the end of 1983, deployment of U.S. missiles would begin. In the light of events, the U.S. administration was suspected of deliberate procrastination, and bad faith was attributed to it. Anxiety about the implications of PIIs and GLCMs on German soil reached extensive proportions and gave impetus to anti-nuclear agitation with a distinctly anti-U.S. flavor. The German peace movement reaped the benefits of this mood as did the Soviet Union, which was not a disinterested party in this matter.

In the United States, the new administration—which had scant knowledge of conditions in the FRG—deplored the unwarranted faith Germans had in arms control and their preoccupation with détente. In effect, in the administration's judgment, the government of the FRG was too eager to appease the Soviet Union and too reluctant to make a greater military contribution to NATO. Bilateral relations between the United States and the FRG deteriorated. They hit a nadir at the end of the first year of the Reagan administration, when martial law was declared in Poland. The reaction of the U.S. government was akin to that of the Carter administration to Afghanistan. The restrained (from a U.S. perspective), almost apologetic stance taken by the German government could not be understood in Washington. Helmut Schmidt appeared the villain, in part because on personal grounds he had not endeared himself to the current occupants of the White House any more than to their predecessors.

Resumption and Breakdown of the INF Talks

Meanwhile, however, primarily through the efforts of Secretary of State Alexander Haig, U.S. opposition to negotiating with the Soviets softened. INF talks began in Geneva on November 30, 1981. The Germans (and other Europeans as well) breathed a sigh of relief. They felt that in Haig they found a friend through whom they could influence U.S. policy. Little did they know how precarious Secretary Haig's position was in the Reagan administration.

The INF talks themselves did not nurture optimism about a favorable (that is, negotiated) outcome. Although a mechanism for consultation among NATO members existed in the form of the Special Consultative Group (headed by Assistant Secretary of State Richard Burt), the FRG government felt that it was kept in the dark about U.S. plans and negotiating strategy. It also felt that its representative, Friedrich Ruth (the foreign ministry's arms control plenipotentiary), exercised little, if any, influence in this forum.

No progress in the talks was registered during the first year. Meanwhile, a change of government took place in the FRG. The social-liberal coalition was replaced by a conservative-liberal grouping. Helmut Kohl, the head of the Christian Democratic Union (CDU), became chancellor replacing the "difficult" Helmut Schmidt. On a subjective level, relations between the United States and the FRG improved. The philosophy and especially the personality of the new German chancellor was more congenial to Americans, although the conservatism of his party was a far cry from the militant, self-confident, and enterprising spirit that characterized the Reagan administration. By comparison, the Germans were timid and unenterprising; they lacked self-confidence and, to some extent, even a sense of identity. In regard to the INF talks, they were genuinely committed to a negotiated agreement and, if anything, were more concerned than the SPD about the domestic repercussions of an extended stalemate and the subsequent stationing of U.S. missiles in the FRG.

Christian Democrats were apprehensive about domestic violence, which would necessitate the use of force against demonstrators and might lead to casualties. Regardless of their convictions about stationing, many CDU members were fearful that their government would not survive a bloody confrontation with anti-nuclear forces. Thus, the conservative-liberal coalition (in which Hans-Dietrich Genscher's position as foreign minister was stronger than ever) fervently wished that the United States would show inclination for compromise in the INF talks. President Reagan's announcement in March 1983 of his modified, interim solution (which the Germans felt reflected exertions they and other Europeans had made) kindled hopes for a possible compromise in the INF talks. On the other hand, the president's Star Wars speech appalled the FRG government, for his moral stance on the elimination of nuclear weapons was, of course, grist for the mill of the anti-nuclear forces then rampant in West Germany.

Carefully graduated Soviet statements throughout the spring and summer of 1983—though palpably unsuited as serious proposals at the negotiating table—nevertheless hinted at a willingness to compromise. Invariably, the general reaction in the FRG (including substantial segments of the government) was hopeful and expectant. As the crucial last round of negotiations in the fall of 1983 approached, the Bonn government felt particularly edgy about being left in the dark concerning U.S. strategy in Geneva and at a loss as to the proper posture it should strike at home. The government was, in a sense, immobilized because of its close ties to the United States and its predisposition to be pliant to U.S. wishes. Somewhat greater independence might have been useful from a domestic political point of view; too close an identification with the United States was not propitious at this time.

Among the issues with which the government had to cope, fear of the consequences of stationing was the most serious. For one thing, there was widespread concern that stationing of U.S. missiles in Europe would give the United States an independent Eurostrategic capacity for the conduct of war on the continent. In other words, decoupling of European defenses from U.S. defenses once again caused fears about the FRG's security, except that this time—in contrast with the 1970s—it was the presence of U.S. medium-range missiles that instilled this concern, not their absence. Also, many Germans were apprehensive about the reaction of the Soviet Union, especially as it might affect relations with the GDR.

Under the conservative-liberal coalition, the pace of improvement in these relations accelerated. The conservatives were beneficiaries of the groundwork that had been painstakingly laid by the social-liberal coalition and they did not want to jeopardize the gains of a decade. Apart from considerations of their own security, West Germans had convinced themselves that they bore a responsibility for their fellow nationals living across the border and should not contribute to the hardships of the East German population.

Much hung in the balance for the FRG for giving renewed and final approval to the stationing of U.S. missiles, but alliance solidarity demanded nothing less. The Bundestag, after a two-day debate on November 21–22, 1983, endorsed stationing by a comfortable margin of votes. The following day, Soviet negotiators walked out on the Geneva talks. The stage for deployment was set. Some adherents of the government felt that the FRG had done what was expected of it. Now the United States could reciprocate by delaying—if not suspending—deployment altogether and, with this signal of good will, could still prevent the onset of a new period of deep freeze in East-West relations.

Such actions did not materialize, but neither did the worst consequences of deployment. Public agitation against deployment subsided. The peace movement was in a refractory state. The GDR—as Chancellor Kohl had bravely predicted—did not interrupt the studied course of piecemeal improvement of relations with the FRG on which it had embarked. In fact, from East Germany came confirmation of a shared interest to avoid confrontation; the GDR appeared as unhappy as the FRG about aggravated East-West relations in Europe. Both regimes seemed intent on creating a sort of oasis of peace in the center of Europe. Among other things, they began to exchange information about arms control and disarmament in periodic meetings between their respective arms control chiefs.

The hiatus in INF talks and other bilateral, U.S.-Soviet arms control negotiations throughout 1984 blighted MBFR discussions as well, although these were not adjourned sine die. Yet the possibility of progress in these talks—despite earlier evidence of rapprochement between the Eastern and Western positions—was dim, if not nonexistent, largely because of the reserved attitude of the United States. Reopening the arms control process in 1985 rekindled expectations in the FRG, and much hope was attached to the Geneva summit between President Reagan and General Secretary Mikhail Gorbachev.

Erosion of Security Policy Consensus in the FRG

In essence little, if anything, has changed during the mid-1980s in the basic outlook on arms control, disarmament, and improved East-

West relations in the FRG. But it is clear that a return to détente at its best—as in the 1970s—is not in the offing.

One consequence of the developments since 1982 has been an erosion (some people claim a breakdown) in the security policy consensus that existed in the FRG throughout the better part of the 1970s. Although the conservative opposition parties viewed the SPD *Ostpolitik* with misgivings in the beginning stages, they ultimately identified with its basic features. When the conservatives returned to rule, after a hiatus of thirteen years, they did not introduce significant changes. Not only did Hans-Dietrich Genscher remain at his post, and thus assure continuity in foreign policy, his position (despite growing criticism from conservative quarters) became even stronger. Actually, a certain differentiation is observable in the conservative-liberal coalition, but without significant impact on the conduct of policy for the time being.

The SPD, however, drifted away from the positions it supported under the chancellorship of Helmut Schmidt. One reason is that Schmidt and individuals with whom he surrounded himself—as, for example, Defense Minister Georg Leber and his successor Hans Apel, but not only they—were essentially moderate persons with a sober sense of national security requirements. Schmidt's commitment to LRTNF modernization was not popular in his party, and a portion of the majority that formally supported him did so largely because it did not want to trade privilege (which accrues to the party in control of the government) for ideological principle. Free of its governmental responsibilities, the SPD quickly distanced itself from Schmidt and became "radicalized" in foreign policy matters. So far, no unity has developed in the party on a foreign and security policy platform. Several individuals and factions are vying to formulate a comprehensive platform and have it accepted by the party as a whole. The general tenor of SPD proposals does not represent a radical break with the past; but it is more emphatic about the necessity of establishing a framework of peace and cooperation in Europe as the environment best suited to safeguard the FRG's security. And the SPD has been openly critical of U.S. policies in Europe in the recent period. In the view of many SPD adherents, the United States is primarily responsible for the lack of common concepts, which in the past few years has consistently worked to the disadvantage of the alliance.

The slogans of the SPD more than the policy content of its proposals have had a disturbing effect on conservatives in the FRG and, of course, in the United States. Slogans such as *Equidistanz* ("equal distance" toward West and East) and *Sicherheitspartnerschaft* ("security partnerships" with the East) seem to carry dire implications. It is necessary to understand their meaning in order to know that they are relatively harmless, although their implementation presupposes and is designed to create—through peaceful processes of interaction, including arms control, disarmament, and confidence building—a climate conducive to East-West cooperation in Europe. The SPD is firmly convinced that peace cannot be secured in Europe without the Soviet Union. The security concerns of the WP states have to be taken into account. Emphasizing only Western security concerns and requirements perpetuates—and under certain circumstances aggravates—an adversary relationship with the East.

The approach taken by the SPD has the earmarks of appeasement, and that is troublesome. But the conservative-liberal coalition, in its majority, is not too far from identical basic premises. Both sides, for reasons of their own, seem to want to emphasize polarization of opinion on foreign and security policy questions for electoral purposes. The government levels exaggerated charges of recklessness and irresponsibility against the SPD and thus seeks to evoke a historical image of that party as unworthy of being entrusted with the destiny of the German state.

To some extent, conservatives are impelled to do this because of their own disability to develop a distinct foreign and security policy as a result of their close affiliation with and dependence on the United States. The SPD, of course, is free of governmental responsibilities and therefore has more latitude for introducing innovations that at times may appear to have merit, while at other times appear to be reckless. The SPD also tends to take advantage of the immobility of the government and seeks to exploit an image of the government as a lackey of the United States.

Conclusion

As for German and U.S. perceptions of arms control, the record of experiences since the late 1960s appears to indicate a divergence rather than a convergence of views. It is impossible to be either inclusive or exhaustive in the treatment of so vast a subject in the compass of a short study. The arms control interests and involvements of both countries are not limited to the negotiations to which reference has been made here, and the evolution of attitudes toward arms control as an instrument of foreign and security policy requires a much more detailed analysis. In general, the following observations may be made: No one appears to have correctly gauged the nuclear arms control process before it was launched. All participants have had to learn in the course of the process. Technical questions—with which Germans on the whole have not been intimately acquainted—have proved to be less tractable than might have been anticipated. The question of mutual trust has been particularly vexing because of factors both intrinsic (arms control and arms competition) and extrinsic (non–arms control issues that face states involved in arms control).

Arms control alone cannot bear the brunt of the burden for easing East-West tensions. It is a mistake to overload it, as it were, for that can contribute to its breakdown. The United States has, on the whole (though more and less under various administrations), held an instrumental view of arms control as one means of conducting the struggle with the Soviet Union. The Reagan administration's position—that arms control, if it must be conducted at all, requires extreme prudence and should be seen as an instrument by which the Soviet Union can be constrained to comply with essentially Western (U.S.) terms of conduct—is somewhat extreme. But all U.S. administrations seem to have viewed arms control from a rather narrow, militaristic vantage; that is, the military component has dominated the content of U.S. arms control strategy.

Because of the global nature of the struggle with the Soviet Union, especially since the beginning of détente, the regional interests of European allies have at times been neglected or underestimated (as, for example—in the view of Germans—by Paul Warnke, one of President Carter's arms control negotiators). Because of superpower preeminence—if not exclusiveness—in nuclear arms, the United States has been disinclined to share information with its allies. (Secretiveness is, of course, ingrained in the Soviet system. It would be unfair to compare the United States with the Soviet Union in this respect.) Finally, the United States basically has been able to safeguard its security interests with or without arms control. At least that appears to have been the dominant attitude in all administrations, although not to an equal degree.

The Germans, by contrast, have not been able to safeguard their security interests. They have been extremely vulnerable and just about totally dependent on the United States as their protective power (*Schutzmacht*). This dependence, which has extended over a long period, has been a source of cumulative frustration and irritation with the United States. Yet as long as an adversary relationship exists between East and West in Europe, the Germans have no practical alternative. The elimination, or at least significant attenuation, of this adversary relationship holds out the best hope for the creation of conditions in which their security would not be threatened without U.S. protection. Arms control is seen by them as an integral element of détente, but they emphasize the political and psychological aspects as having significance equal to—if not greater than—strictly military considerations.

Clearly, the points of departure toward arms control are considerably at variance between the United States and the Federal Republic of Germany. Germans have ample, if often self-induced, reasons for imputing motives to the United States which in fact the United States does not have. Basically, they are insecure about U.S. intentions. Their insecurity is in part a function of the diminished and diminishing capability of the United States to offer them foolproof protection, and that without risking its own security.

The Soviet Union's massive military effort has changed the conditions of existence of the Western alliance. In the view of the Germans, who for long clung to the model of adversary relations, recognition of the imperatives of the changed conditions would suggest cooperation in Europe. Conflict does not accord with their interests, and armed conflict would threaten their very survival.

Notes

1. In his memoirs, H. Kissinger notes that "as soon as we set a date for the opening of SALT and began briefing our allies, they began to grasp the strategic implications. An agreement between the Soviet Union and the United States to limit strategic weapons would inevitably ratify strategic equality. There could be no other basis for negotiation; and indeed our briefings point out to them that parity was approaching even *without* agreement as a result of the steady growth of Soviet forces (italics in original)." Henry Kissinger, *White House Years* (Boston: Little, Brown, 1979), p. 404.

2. See my discussion "Problems and Prospects of Troop Reductions in Central Europe," especially p. 33, in Paul E. Zinner, *East-West Relations in Europe: Observations and Advice from the Sidelines, 1971-1982* (Boulder, Colo.: Westview Press, 1984).

3. Reinhard Mutz, ed., *Die Wiener Verhandlungen über Truppenreduzierungen in Mitteleuropa (MBFR)* (Baden-Baden: Nomos, 1983), p. 44.

4. Ibid., p. 45.

5. Lothar Ruehl, "Belastungen des amerikanisch-europäischen Verhältnisses," in Wolfgang Wagner et al., *Die Internationale Politik, 1979/1980* (Munich and Vienna: Oldenbourg Verlag, 1983), p. 50.

6. In his memoirs, President Carter's national security advisor disparages Chancellor Helmut Schmidt on several occasions. See Zbigniew Brzezinski, *Power and Principle* (New York: Farrar, Strauss, Giroux, 1983), especially pp. 307 and 463.

7. Chancellor Schmidt's speech was printed in *Survival* (London: International Institute for Strategic Studies, vol. 20, January/February 1978), pp. 2-10; also in Wolfram F. Hanrieder, ed., *Helmut Schmidt: Perspectives on Politics* (Boulder, Colo.: Westview Press, 1982), pp. 23-37.

8. Interview given by Helmut Schmidt in *Frankfurter Rundschau*, December 12, 1982.

9. Walther Stützle, *Politik und Kräfteverhältnis* (Herford: E. S. Mittler, 1983), p. 157.

10. Brzezinski, op. cit., p. 308.

11. "Dokumente zum Besuch des deutschen Bundeskanzlers in Moskau am 30 Juni und 1 Juli 1980," *Europa Archiv*, vol. 35, no. 15 (August 10, 1980): D425-444.

12. Brzezinski, op. cit., p. 309.

13. See Hartmut Wasser, "Die USA in der 'Ära der nationalen Erneuerung' unter Ronald Reagan," in *Die Internationale Politik, 1981/1982*, pp. 2-20.

Bibliography

There is a voluminous literature on the subject matter covered in this article. In addition to the sources quoted in footnotes, I found the following books most useful:

Forndran, Erhard, and Paul J. Friedrich, eds. *Rüstungsbeschränkung und Sicherheit*. Bonn: Union Verlag, 1979.

Füllenbach, Josef, and Eberhard Schulz, eds. *Entspannung am Ende?* Munich and Vienna: Oldenbourg Verlag, 1980.

Haftendorn, Helga. *Abrüstungs- und Entspannungspolitik zwischen Sicherheitsbefriedigung und Friedenssicherung; Zur Aussenpolitik der BRD 1955-1973*. Düsseldorf: Bertelsmann Universitätsverlag, 1974.

Kaiser, Karl, and Hans-Peter Schwarz, eds. *America and Western Europe: Problems and Prospects*. Lexington, Ky.: Lexington Books, 1977.

Kaiser, Karl, and Karl Markus Kreis, eds. *Sicherheitspolitik vor neuen Aufgaben*. Bonn: Europa Union Verlag, 1977.

3

The Evolution of West German Public Opinion on Détente Since 1970

Peter H. Merkl

It is a truism to say that there has been an erosion of sorts in the support of West German public opinion for some key aspects of U.S. defense policy since the early 1970s. But it is not at all easy to spell out just what has changed and why. Many relevant indicators of West German support for the most important ally of the Federal Republic have not changed at all, or have only fluctuated in various ways. U.S. policymakers and media have always tended to view vacillations of views of an ally in such a black-and-white fashion—"Are they for us or against us?"—that any attempt at analysis must first spell out briefly some of the baffling complexities of the FRG's international situation before proceeding to a detailed examination of the evidence.

To begin with, Germany is a divided country, the western part of which is still linked to Communist Eastern Germany by sentiment, tradition, and an astonishing volume of trade. These ties were present in some form even before the building of the Berlin Wall in 1961 and they grew even stronger with the agreements of the early and mid-1970s such as the Basic Treaty, and the establishment of government-level relations, if not diplomatic recognition, between Bonn and the GDR. These ties inhibit the Federal Republic's willingness to respond to every turn in the global East-West confrontation (Bonn for example, will shield inner-German trade from economic sanctions) and make the Federal Republic more vulnerable than other allies to tensions between the two Germanys, such as over East German spy scandals in Bonn, the fortunately less frequent border disruptions, and Berlin crises of past decades. These ties also give the GDR a special status within the Communist bloc.[1]

Secondly, quite unlike France or Great Britain, the Federal Republic is situated directly at the edge of the Iron Curtain and astride the most likely Warsaw Pact invasion route in the event of a conventional war. West Germans are well aware of their vulnerability to any East-West clash in Europe, conventional or tactical nuclear, and they know that their country would most likely be quickly overrun or turned into a devastated battlefield before they might benefit from their NATO alliance. They also know, especially now, that the presence of large numbers of NATO military installations and missile sites makes them targets of Soviet intermediate-range nuclear missiles and that attack would probably mean, in their Oregon-sized country, death for most of their civilian population. These circumstances have introduced profound ambiguities into German public attitudes toward defense, perhaps even a kind of escapism, a desire especially of the younger generations to "opt out" of this perilous situation if possible. Young Germans like to point to neutral Switzerland as if it were possible to remove Germany from the shooting range of the Cold War to a quiet corner of the world. They are extremely uneasy with the geopolitical situation in which World War II left their country.

For the older generations, too, the exposed position of West Germany at the edge of the East-West conflict in Europe has generated ambiguous feelings and, perhaps, a somewhat manipulative approach to Western defense. On the one hand, their idea of external security for the Federal Republic is likely to stress the maintenance of peace by almost any means that promise to forestall armed conflict on their territory: alliances, deterrence, guarantees, and especially East-West agreements and negotiations that reduce the level of tensions. On the other hand, they do become rather nervous at saber-rattling threats and loose talk of European armed conflict whether it comes from Washington or Moscow. West Germans have little sympathy for a policy of military strength, or buildup, preferring instead notions of approximate military balance,[2] and the mutual de-escalation of aggressive rhetoric. Since the 1960s, they have preferred a policy of "live and let live" between East and West to ideological confrontations. Nuclear weapons, in their view, have a mostly political function—deterrence, which is seen strictly as a defensive strategy. Any thought of actually using nuclear weapons, or even merely making them operational, makes West Germans blanch. And although a growing majority of West Germans say now that they would "rather fight than accept Soviet domination,"[3] the numbers insisting on avoiding nuclear war at all costs have always been far higher than in the United States.[4] In West German eyes the credibility of Western leadership and military strategy depends on its avoidance of nuclear war, not on tough talk or ideological crusades.

The third factor in the West German situation that distinguishes German from U.S. views is the European option. Even if it seems a questionable guarantee of West German security, we must remember that century-old traditions and long-standing economic and political involvement with the European Community (EC) determine most nondefense foreign policies of the Federal Republic. When U.S. leadership of the Western alliance is perceived as faltering or inept, and when U.S. economic and monetary policies are seen as selfish or exploitive of the nations of Western Europe, the question of a European option—perhaps a French-led defensive union or a European currency—is likely to arise. Germans may have less reason to trust an independent European defense but they also have been more inclined to invest their hopes in the idea of European union than have the other members of the European Community. Since the beginnings of *Ostpolitik* and of the Helsinki negotiations, moreover, some Germans have even considered their sense of European community to include Eastern European nations as well.[5]

Recent West German public opinion polls clearly reflect the extent of this European identification. When asked in March 1979 what concepts they associated with the European community, 84 percent of a representative cross section of West Germans named the "future," 79 percent "peace," and 73 percent "security,"[6] even though the EC currently has no jurisdiction over defense functions. Between 69 percent and 73 percent in polls from 1970 to 1979 said they favored expanding the EC into a political community, presumably of a federal or confederate organization.[7] When asked more specifically if they would accept "a European government responsible for a common policy in foreign affairs, defense, and the economy," however, only 45 percent said yes (no: 31 percent) in 1979, down from 58 percent yes and 22 percent no in 1971, in the early days of *Ostpolitik*. They split evenly for (39 percent) and against (40 percent) a European currency, down from 57 percent for and 22 percent against in 1974, which may have reflected a reaction to the first oil shock. An amazing 64 percent, however, believed "that the security of the Federal Republic will be strengthened in a United Europe."[8] Perhaps the year 1979 was unusual in this respect, but these percentages hardly show a decline of "European sentiment" in the Federal Republic.

Also in the same March 1979 poll, 25 percent of the respondents expressed a desire to see the Soviet Union and the Eastern European countries included in a united Europe while 56 percent wanted to restrict it to Western European countries.[9] This extraordinary result among a rather well informed population demonstrates graphically the limits of placing the Federal Republic strictly into the Western alignment of the East-West conflict, even within the European context. The concept of a Europe from the Atlantic to the Ural Mountains is also notable for what it excludes from the European family of nations: the United States, Canada, Australia, and New Zealand.

The Fever Thermometer

U.S. citizens trying to comprehend the difference between the tough West German defense attitudes of the Adenauer era and the vacillations evident today usually look for a "softening up" or generational change during the years of détente, the 1970s.[10] Though not implausible, this is difficult to demonstrate with public opinion polls because it would make little sense to ask respondents outright whether the period of détente affected their views. There are other ways of comparing the present views with those of earlier eras of West German history. In 1971, I suggested a circuitous route for approaching the attitudinal dimensions of West German distrust of the international system because, on most fundamental questions, positivistic political science is either unable or too timid to ask the relevant questions.

Basically, for historical reasons, West Germans were still very much in the grip of deep-seated and partly irrational fears in the 1950s and early 1960s that focused on the perceived likelihood of a major war—presumably on German territory—and on images of a Soviet threat that were continually reinforced by crises over Berlin, specific Soviet threats against West Germany (such as "turning it into a veritable cemetery" [Khrushchev]), *Sputnik* (1957), and the invasion of Hungary in 1956. These fears began to diminish in the 1960s as a new generation came of age and memories of the air raids and destruction of the 1940s had faded. With the advent of *Ostpolitik,* especially the liberal–social democratic version,[11] and the mutual renunciation-of-force treaties, West Germans learned to relax their fear of war or military attack from the East even though there were other international crises and some economic ones, relating to enery and the monetary system.[12] When asked in 1980 whether they expected the Polish crisis or the invasion of Afghanistan to trigger war, 20 percent saw a real threat or danger of war as a result of the former and 56 percent as a result of the latter, although not necessarily involving Germany.[13]

As reported in 1971, the shadow of World War II still hung so heavily over the West Germans in the 1950s and up until the mid-1960s that between 35 and 45 percent consistently expected another major war in their lifetimes, and 8 to 18 percent even within the next three or four years.[14] In the 1970s, except for the war scares of 1980, this level of fear declined and comfortable majorities were convinced that "no one will risk a world war" (Table 3.1).[15]

Table 3.1 Fear of Major War, 1961–1981 (in percent)

Do you feel we must reckon with another world war, or do you think no one will ever risk a large-scale war again?

	Sept. 1961	June 1967	Dec. 1975	Nov. 1979	May 1980	Jan. 1981
Must reckon with world war	46	38	29	32	37	34
No one will risk world war	45	54	63	59	54	59
Impossible to say	9	8	8	9	9	7
	100%	100%	100%	100%	100%	100%

Source: Elisabeth Noelle-Neumann, ed., *The Germans: Public Opinion Polls, 1967–1980,* rev. ed. (Westport, Conn.: Greenwood Press, 1981), p. 490, and *Comparative Political Studies* 3: 458.

A second question we cited in 1971 was, "Do you think that people who marry and set up a family can face the future with equanimity, or must they be constantly afraid of another war?" Here the pessimistic responses of 35 percent to 45 percent (1961–1968) dropped to 27 percent in 1971 while the optimistic responses jumped from 21–29 percent to 42–62 percent in the 1970s.[16] In any case, the level of fear was still considerable even though there appears to have been a noticeable shift toward economic worries. Fear, rational or irrational, rises and falls like the mercury in a fever thermometer whenever circumstances lend it greater plausibility. But even at its lowest level, fear indicates a level of deep distrust of the international system.

Détente and the Soviet Image

Fears are not irrational if they are clearly linked to a threatening enemy although it may be difficult to say how accurate the perception of a given threat may be or whether historical guilt feelings may aggravate the level of fear.[17] In 1971, opinion polls of the 1950s and 1960s were used to show how the West German perception of a Soviet threat had slowly declined from a level of 64–66 percent who felt threatened in the early 1950s (when 15–21 percent did not) to 38–39 percent in the mid-1960s (37 percent did not in 1964 and 1966).[18] After the beginnings

Table 3.2 Soviet Threatening Image, 1952–1980 (in percent)
Does Russia threaten or does it not threaten us?

	1952	1958	1964	1971	1976	1980
Yes	66	51	39	28	47	44
Undecided	19	22	24	26	15	22
No	15	27	37	46	38	34
	100%	100%	100%	100%	100%	100%

Source: Elisabeth Noelle-Neumann, ed., *The Germans: Public Opinion Polls, 1967–1980*, rev. ed. (Westport, Conn.: Greenwood Press, 1981), p. 430, and *Comparative Political Studies* 3: 459.

of *Ostpolitik*, the perceived Soviet threat dropped further to 28 percent in 1971 (46 percent did not feel threatened) but then increased through the mid-1970s. The percentage of those not viewing the Soviets as a threat increased in the 1970s compared to the 1950s but is still far from the majority.

The responses are discriminating and yet reveal a constant of skepticism over time. After the Soviet Union invaded Afghanistan, a poll revealed a steep increase (from 25 percent in 1977 to 61 percent in January 1980) of West Germans whose opinion of the USSR had "gotten worse in the last two or three years."[19] In any case, the threatening image of the Soviet Union was the major chord that sounded through the tones of peace and reconciliation of the entire era. Throughout the years of détente in the 1970s, a steady 52–59 percent of West Germans maintained that they had "no reason to distrust Russia less today than years ago" and only a fourth or third (26–34 percent) claimed, in deference to the new *Ostpolitik*, that "a lot has changed in Russia since [Stalin's time]."[20] Similar steadfastness, if somewhat softened during the 1970s, kept between 28 and 33 percent insisting from 1955 through 1980 that European democratic freedom was to be defended against Soviet conquest "with every means at our disposal . . . even if it leads to nuclear war," while 40–50 percent preferred to "avoid war above all, even though it means having to live under a communist government." In 1955 and 1960 only 36–38 percent wanted to avoid war at all cost—"better red than dead"—and there were more undecideds than in the 1970s. The anticipation of a Soviet challenge to German security is highlighted further by the perception of Soviet military superiority throughout the years from 1976 to 1981; 46–49 percent considered the East more powerful than the West (in 1976 it was even 57 percent) while no more than 5–7 percent believed the opposite.[21] Behind these judgments, in other words, there was a sense of helpless inferiority.

Nevertheless, in 1970, when the West German policy of détente began in earnest, public opinion polls revealed a new German mood, a readiness for drastic change in foreign policy vis-à-vis the East. This found expression in the acceptance, by large majorities, of statements such as

> 25 years after the war, we have to make a clean break with the past. If we want to get anywhere in politics, we have to deal with the situation as it is [51 percent agreed completely, 24 percent partly].
>
> For 20 years, nothing was done about détente with the East. It's about time that something happened [45 percent agreed completely, 25 percent partly].[22]

The West German refusal to recognize the Oder-Neisse line as the Polish-German border, long a sacred cow of politics in the Adenauer era, suddenly was reversed in the public opinion polls, from a mere 8 percent versus 80 percent for recognition in 1951 to 22 percent versus 59 percent in 1964 to 62 percent versus 18 percent in 1972.[23] This reversal resulted from the popular support of Willy Brandt in 1972 after his government had initiated a package of treaties with Eastern European nations and, by implication, accepted all the German borders in the East.[24] In the same year the first of the renunciation-of-force treaties, with Poland, was endorsed by 43 percent of the public (versus 24 percent). Nevertheless, disappointment was not far behind. By 1973, 45 percent (versus 9 percent who said the opposite) claimed that the Soviet Union had benefited more from improved German-Soviet relations than did West Germany and these numbers changed to 55 percent versus 6 percent by 1980. Thirty-eight to forty percent expressed general disappointment in *Ostpolitik* between 1974 and 1980, and in 1974, 57 percent (versus 22 percent) were keenly disappointed in the whole set of *Ostpolitik* treaties with the Soviet Union, Poland, Czechoslovakia, and East Germany.[25] Nevertheless, in 1973 and 1980, 49–51 percent (versus 29 percent) agreed that negotiations with the Eastern countries still were "worth the effort," and in 1980, 74 percent (versus 17 percent) believed that the policy of détente should be continued. By 1977, a clear majority of 61 percent (as compared to 19 percent of the opposite view) complained that "the Russians take advantage of our good will in the matter of reconciliation with the East." In the same crisis year, under the shadow of the invasion of Afghanistan, 78 percent (versus 9 percent) said that "Europe and especially West Germany should continue détente . . . and that the West use all the means at its disposal to prevent a return to the Cold War."[26]

Perceptions of the United States as an Ally

Within a year, however, an administration profoundly hostile to détente had taken office in Washington and this change soon produced a strong reaction—the Peace Movement—in the German public. The public opinion data reviewed here clearly show why. Far from having developed a false sense of security during the 1970s, West Germans had a fairly realistic picture of their complex situation. They could hardly help being alarmed by the aggressiveness of the rhetoric and the obvious lack of understanding for the German dilemmas in Washington.[27]

From the first year of the Reagan presidency (1981), West Germany's Peace Movement suddenly became very active again, after decades of quiet, and there have been massive demonstrations against the U.S. president, other U.S. officials, and the stationing of Pershing IIs and cruise missiles in the Federal Republic. To be sure, blaming the President or the United States for the nuclear rearmament of NATO forces was neither accurate nor fair because the West German chancellor, Helmut Schmidt, had played a major role in the 1979 "double-track" decision and the Reagan administration inherited the policy from its predecessor. From 1976 West Germans also showed a notable readiness to support a reinforcement of NATO troops, presumably because of the perceived weakness of the West: from 25 percent for reinforcement (versus 36 percent against) in 1971 there grew a plurality for reinforcement in 1976 (41:20 percent) and 1979 (38:24 percent) and, finally, in 1980 a majority of 50 percent (versus 25 percent).[28]

A question about deployment was asked in 1979 before the issue of the missiles had become such an emotional bone of contention: 38 percent approved (34 percent did not) the deployment of U.S. medium-range missiles to counter Soviet medium-range SS-20s.[29] Nevertheless, Reagan himself was a factor as soon as he appeared on the national stage. During the presidential campaign in 1980, far fewer West German respondents rated him well qualified (only 10 percent) than rated Jimmy Carter (43 percent) or Senator Edward Kennedy (23 percent) so. Moreover, their liking for him as a person was no clue to whether they considered him "good for Germany": Although 36 percent said they liked the man, only 27 percent thought that he was "good for Germany."[30]

Indeed, a personal liking is not the same as support for a person's or a foreign nation's policy. In our 1971 report, we contrasted the percentages of West Germans who said they "liked Americans" (39 percent in 1957, 54 percent in 1962) with the 81 percent who supported collaboration with the U.S. government. In spite of much misleading talk of growing anti-Americanism, about the same percentages (42–51 percent) continued to express a personal liking for Americans throughout the 1960s and 1970s, and the same 19–24 percent said they did not particularly like Americans.[31] But the real point is that, personal likes and dislikes aside, the desire for cooperating with the U.S. government continued at the 80 percent level all the way through the early 1980s. The cooperation curve for the Soviets, on the other hand, has changed.[32] Beginning at a level of around 20 percent in the 1950s, it rose in the 1960s to a high point of over 50 percent in 1970 only to decline again through the 1970s to a low point of 20 percent in 1980. In the early 1980s it rose again, possibly in reaction to Moscow's passivity under three moribund leaders.

By comparison, President Reagan's "political actions, all in all" during the period of the surging West German Peace Movement (1981–1983) were judged in a rising curve as "too hard"—25:2 percent in May 1981, 38:2 percent in September/October 1981, 38:4 percent in December 1981, 47:4 percent in October/November 1982, and 40:6 percent in June 1983. On the other hand, the question, "Do you have overall a good or not so good opinion of Reagan?" produced considerable fluctuations. After a brief headstart of positive views in May and July 1981, when he had visited Berlin and Bonn, there were steadily more "not so good" opinions until, from mid-1982 to mid-1983, majorities of two to one (45–51 percent versus 18–24 percent) expressed disapproval.[33] The coup de grâce was delivered by the response to a May 1981 question, "How confident are you that the United States is capable of taking a wise leadership role today?" Forty-two percent answered "very" or "fairly confident" while 47 percent said "not so" or "not at all confident." On this question generational differences were noticeable; those forty-five or older, especially those over fifty-nine years, were more confident of U.S. leadership, which evidently they remembered more positively from the earlier decades of the Federal Republic.[34]

West German Options

What is West Germany to do for her security if U.S. leadership and strength are faltering? One option is détente between East and West, and we have already reviewed the continuing West German support for it. Another is to stand by the United States despite the impression of weakness and weak leadership. A third option is cooperation with the Soviet Union, but this clearly attracts only a tiny minority (Table 3.3). The most interesting choice is "to cooperate equally with the U.S. and the Soviet Union," and in the polls this option—whatever it may mean in operational terms—even enjoyed a majority of support in 1973, which it lost again by the end of the decade to the option of standing by the United States. The two options still vie for majorities today.

Table 3.3 Neutrality Versus Close Cooperation with the United States (in percent)

Should the Federal Republic cooperate equally with both, more closely with the United States, or more closely with the USSR?

	1965	1973	1977	1978	1980	1981
Equal cooperation with both	37	54	38	36	41	32
Closer with U.S.	46	36	49	51	49	56
Closer with USSR	—	3	2	1	2	1
Undecided	—	7	11	12	8	11
	83%	100%	100%	100%	100%	100%

Source: Elisabeth Noelle-Neumann, ed., *The Germans: Public Opinion Polls, 1967–1980*, rev. ed. (Westport, Conn.: Greenwood Press, 1981), p. 415, and *Comparative Political Studies* 3: 462. The first column shows the results of a question asking whether respondents thought Germany should "go neutral" or "stay with the U.S./West."

There are several possible interpretations of the idea of equal cooperation with both sides. One of them assumes peaceful coexistence between East and West and it is remarkable that, by 1979 and 1981, majorities thought peaceful coexistence possible.[35] Given coexistence, the Federal Republic could lead an undisturbed life between the two, but would it have to drop out of NATO or perhaps even out of the European Community? A May 1980 question provided something of a "reasonableness" test by juxtaposing two positions, one of loyalty to U.S. policies in other parts of the world and the other proposing "a solid front with the Americans as far as possible; but if they establish policies that are unreasonable, they can't expect us to go along with measures that run counter to our own interests." The second position attracted 49 percent and a majority of adherents of the SPD and FDP while the loyalist opinion only received 39 percent, including a majority of the Christian Democratic Union/Christian Social Union (CDU/CSU) supporters. A year later, while President Reagan visited Germany, moreover, the same question drew 68 percent who insisted on U.S. "reasonableness" versus only 20 percent of loyalists.[36] Among the issues that West Germans may have found less reasonable were Vietnam, current policies toward Central America and the Third World in general, and economic sanctions against Eastern or Third World trading partners.

Whatever becoming a neutral state may imply, the notion still seems to conjure up old West German fears of becoming "isolated and not able to resist Soviet pressure." Hence, broad majorities of 63–64 percent opted for the West in polls taken in late 1981 and late 1984 (versus 35 percent neutralists). Predictably these majorities were even more ample (77–79 percent) among the Christian and Free Democratic adherents in 1984, while the SPD was closer to an even split between 45 percent for neutrality and 55 percent for alliance with the West. Only supporters of the new Green party overwhelmingly (73 percent) backed the neutralists.[37] But this position is hardly the majority sentiment nor is the Green party position on West German membership in NATO: In August 1983, 51 percent of Green supporters wanted the Federal Republic to leave NATO, versus 28 percent who did not. A majority of 72 percent of the adult population preferred staying in NATO, however, including 81–86 percent of the adherents of CDU/CSU and FDP. Even SPD supporters backed it 68 percent to 12 percent, which leads one to wonder what three-fourths of the 45 percent SPD supporters who advocated West German neutralism could have had in mind.[38] Could there be a neutralist option for the Federal Republic without leaving NATO? Surprising turns of course are not impossible. In 1979, a question proposed the following scenario for German reunification: West and East Germany must withdraw from NATO and the Warsaw Pact, respectively, while the neutrality of a reunited Germany would be guaranteed and its choice of a social system determined by free elections. Forty-nine percent said they would welcome such a solution (26 percent would not), but only 17 percent thought it possible (64 percent did not).[39]

After the pacifist upheaval of 1981–1983, even the stationing of the new nuclear medium-range missiles found increased support (Table 3.4). There were pluralities of 40–42 percent in the years of anti-missile agitation—until the deployment actually began in late 1983—who saw in it a measure of assured peace, but a year later they grew to 48 percent while the temporary surge of pacifist sentiment returned to the level of 1982 (from 28 percent to 22 percent). The difference between the two sides, of course, was a matter of perceiving the missiles as increasing or decreasing the likelihood of attack upon the Federal Republic.

Because the peace movement is supported predominantly by involved young people under 25, it is even more revealing to break down the responses in the years 1983 and 1984 for the 16–24 year olds. Table 3.4 clearly shows that the fearful 1983 majority among the young receded in 1984 when the young differed only a little from the population at large on this issue.[40]

Another question of the same year ascertained that 61 percent of the respondents still associated nuclear weapons predominantly with deter-

Table 3.4 Nuclear Rearmament and Security (in percent)

What do you think about the development of new nuclear weapons for Western Europe? Did this increase the likelihood of an attack, or is our security improved by this development?

	1982	1983	1984	16–24 Year Olds 1983	1984
Likelihood of attack greater	22	28	22	54	26
Security is improved by development	42	40	48	18	42
No difference	32	28	28	25	30
Undecided	3	4	1	3	2
	100%	100%	100%	100%	100%

Source: Verteidigungsklima 1972–1983 (Emnid, 1983).

rence against conventional attack. Another 37 percent remained unreconciled to the thirty-year presence of nuclear weapons on both sides and would have preferred to get rid of them.[41] In this respect, of course, they are the true descendants of the ban-the-bomb marchers of 1957 when public opinion polls revealed even higher levels (72 percent) of West Germans opposed to arming the *Bundeswehr* with nuclear weapons. Many of those expressing apprehensions about nuclear weapons, however, did not hesitate to point to their deterrence value toward the Soviet threat.[42] It would be simplistic indeed to press these complex divisions into a simple pro-U.S. versus anti-U.S. mold. Many Germans, especially the young, simply are not very anxious to die an atomic death and will not even change their minds for our sakes.

Conclusion

It may be appropriate at this point to summarize and look back upon the path we have traveled. We began by spelling out three crucial factors of West Germany's international situation that make it unique: the German division, vulnerability to an East-West clash in Europe, and relationship to the European context. However loyal an ally, the Federal Republic is obviously constrained by these strategic factors and can hardly be expected to respond to every international crisis as any part of this country would. The most striking manifestation of the first two of these factors is the still surprisingly high level of West German fears of fatal involvement in a major war. The curve of these fears made over recent decades inversely reflects drops in the temperature of the cold war and its most recent return. Surging fears of war may have seemingly contradictory effects on West German minds: On the one hand, they may suggest close adherence to the Western alliance and its tough deterrent posture in the hope that this policy might avert the dreaded coming of war to German soil. On the other hand, the fear of major war could just as well counsel eager negotiations with the East, major measures of détente, neutralism, and even surrender to the feared enemy: Better Red than dead. Given the uncertainties of the alliance, the ambiguity of their situation may lead West German leaders and the public to vacillate or to combine tough talk with a considerable willingness to yield when the chips are down.[43]

The changing perceptions of the Soviet threat to West Germany during the years before and after the heyday of *Ostpolitik* faithfully mirror the declining (though still high) level of distrust of Soviet intentions before and during the years that are sometimes described as the softening-up process of détente. There was a noticeable if brief moment of exhilarating hope among the West German public for lasting reconciliation with the East, though it soon gave way to disappointment with particular *Ostpolitik* measures and, by the second half of the 1970s, to a gradual return to cold war postures. And all through the flowering of détente sentiments, there was a level of distrust of long-range Soviet intentions that makes it difficult to maintain that the West Germans were lulled into a false sense of security by the years of the thaw in the cold war.

Given the lapse of West German awareness of the Soviet threat during the 1970s, how can we explain the peace demonstrations, the anti-missile protests, and the "anti-Americanism" of the early 1980s? Clearly we need to look also at West German attitudes toward the United States and the Western alliance, taking care to avoid confusing a personal like or dislike for Americans or a particular U.S. president with West German readiness to cooperate with the U.S. defense posture and with NATO. As it turns out, West German willingness to augment NATO militarily had actually been on the rise in the late 1970s—before the onset of the peace demonstrations of 1981–1983—and West German reliance on the presence of U.S. troops in Germany was never higher. The popularity of Americans in the Federal Republic has remained virtually unchanged and so have the high (80 percent) levels of German eagerness to stay in NATO and to cooperate with the Western defense effort. With the sole exception of Green party supporters, the overwhelming majority of West Germans never wavered in their support for NATO—not even neutralists who support the SPD. The upwelling of pacifist sentiment at the beginning of the 1980s seems to darken into an enigma.

There are several clues that need to be considered in the context of the three peculiarities of the German situation that I mentioned at the outset: One is the overwhelming conviction among West Germans that the United States and the Western alliance have become so weak as to be no match for Soviet power, at least in the context of a conventional attack on Germany. Add to this the fluctuating perceptions of weak or "unreasonable" U.S. leadership of the alliance, and cast them into scenarios of East-West conflicts in distant theaters or of dubious U.S. policies toward Third World countries (Central America), to dramatize the frequent differences between West German and U.S. foreign policy interests. Add, perhaps, also the increase in intermediate and tactical nuclear weapons in Europe and the increase of talk in Washington of the possibility of a limited nuclear confrontation—perhaps in Europe. Can we really blame young Germans when they reacted with nervous jitters to the Reagan formula of combining the Western position of evident weakness with ideological confrontations with the "evil empire"? A country that is directly in the line of fire between East and West, geographically and by dint of its division and links to Communist East Germany, must feel particularly exposed to the dangers of the East-West conflict, and never more so than when the SS-20s and new NATO intermediate-range missiles are facing off over its soil.

By the mid-1980s, nevertheless, the nervousness of the protests against the deployment of the missiles subsided again. The conviction that the new NATO missiles might help secure the peace rather than endanger it has reached even the restless young Germans who were so profoundly alarmed in 1982–1983. The U.S. president and the Soviet Communist leader have actually met and begun to negotiate—as the original NATO double-track decision had promised in 1979 and as the peace protesters had been demanding for years—a potential loosening of the military-technological noose around Central Europe. West German opinion about the foreign policy options open to their country has also reverted to the consensus that had animated NATO during its first two decades: The neutralist option, or the vague notion of "German equidistance" between the two power blocs, which had been so strong in the early 1970s, now runs again a distant second place behind West German reliance on partnership with NATO and with the United States. Even nuclear weapons, despite some deep-seated misgivings, again are seen as helping to revive the posture of deterrence against an attack from the East, whether conventional or nuclear.[44] Brave words spoken into the ill winds from the East once more have helped to calm the gnawing fears that the Federal Republic has inherited from history and geography.

Notes

1. See Hansjurgen Schierbaum, *Intra-German Relations, Development, Problems, Facts* (Munich: Tuduv, 1979). See also Melvin Croan, "Dilemmas of Ostpolitik," and Richard Kunz, "German Ostpolitik: Its Goals and Foundations," in Peter H. Merkl, ed., *West German Foreign Policy: Dilemmas and Directions* (Chicago: Council on Foreign Relations, 1983), pp. 35–62. Equally unusual for a Communist satellite, of course, is the penetration of the GDR by millions of West German tourists every year (often visiting relatives) and by West German television, which can be seen in nearly all parts of the GDR.

2. As Peter Schmidt pointed out in his paper "Public Opinion and Security in West Germany" (Sept. 1984), interviews with West German security elites have shown a far lower level of conviction that "military strength" is important to West German national security than was the case with their French and American equivalents. On the toughening of U.S. views, see Tom W. Smith, "The Polls, American Attitudes Toward the Soviet Union and Communism," *Public Opinion Quarterly*, 47 (1983): pp. 277ff. and Robert W. Oldendick and Barbara A. Bardes, "Mass and Elite Foreign Policy Opinions," *Public Opinion Quarterly*, 46 (1982): 374–375.

3. See *Verteidigungsklima 1972–1983* (Emnid, 1983): From 42 percent in 1975, those who "would react to an armed conventional attack by taking up arms" grew to 61 percent in 1983.

4. Forty-eight percent of West Germans in 1981 (up from 42 percent in 1975) expressed this view as compared to 32 percent of Americans in 1982. See *Public Opinion*, Aug./Sept. 1981 and April/May 1983. In a Berlin study comparing security elites, the West Germans stood out among a sampling of their French, British, Dutch, and U.S. equivalents with 37 percent who felt that "military force should never be used" (compared to only 4 percent of Americans and 6–9 percent of the others) and another 18 percent who felt that "nuclear weapons could never be justified," not even in the case of a nuclear attack (compared to 14 percent of the Americans, none of the French, 31 percent of the British, and 25 percent of the Dutch security elites). Quoted by Schmidt, "Public Opinion and Security." This level of abhorrence of nuclear war was already present in the Federal Republic in the 1950s.

5. This concept of a Western and Eastern European concert of nations, the Gaullist vision of a "Europe of fatherlands" from the Atlantic to the Ural Mountains, of course, also can be traced back through centuries of European history before the Russian revolution of 1917, or certainly before 1939. See also Peter Schmidt, "Europeanization of Defense: Prospect of Consensus?" Rand Paper (Santa Monica, Calif.: Rand Corporation, December 7, 1984).

6. Elisabeth Noelle-Neumann, ed., *The Germans: Public Opinion Polls, 1967–1980*. Institut für Demoskopie Allensbach (Westport, Conn.: Greenwood Press, 1981), p. 438. Eight percent, 11 percent, and 15 percent, respectively, rejected those answers. All of the percentages cited are of a representative sample of people in the FRG and West Berlin over the age of fifteen.

7. The percentage opting for a political federation or confederation of European governments increased from 68 percent in 1970 to 76 percent in 1979. Ibid., p. 440.

8. Ibid., pp. 442–443. On the last question, 17 percent thought that the presence of Communists in the European institutions—such as the European parliament about to be elected later that year—would undermine West German security, and 19 percent were undecided.

9. Ibid., p. 439. Nineteen percent were undecided.

10. See Stephen Szabo, "The New Generation: Protest and Postmaterialism," in R. G. Livingston, ed., *The Federal Republic in the 1980s* (New York: German Information Center, 1983), pp. 31–42. In the media version, the contrast is painted in cruder strokes, for example, by contrasting the German militarism of old and the Allied demilitarization policy of 1945—"many thought it hopeless"—with today's unmilitaristic Germans. See Konrad Kellen, "The New Germans," *New York Times Magazine*, Aug. 5, 1984, p. 18.

11. For details see Peter H. Merkl, *German Foreign Policies, West and East: On the Threshold of a New European Era* (Santa Barbara, Calif.: Clio Press, 1974), Chapters 5 and 6. The first era of détente already occurred in the 1960s with arms limitations, test bans, and an abortive attempt at *Ostpolitik* in 1967–1968.

12. Asked about "their greatest worries and difficulties at the moment" in January 1980, 18 percent mentioned war and such international crises as oil and Afghanistan, up from 1 percent in April 1972, on the eve of the submission of the renunciation-of-force treaties to parliament. Noelle-Neumann, *The Germans,* p. 103.

13. Ibid., pp. 462 and 478. In 1974, at a time of heightened Sino-Russian tensions, 8 percent of West Germans believed there would be a war between the two countries while 61 percent did not think so. Ibid., p. 473.

14. Peter H. Merkl, "Politico-Cultural Restraints on West German Foreign Policy: Sense of Trust, Identity, and Agency," *Comparative Political Studies* 3 (Jan. 1971): 458.

15. Ibid. and Noelle-Neumann, *The Germans,* p. 490.

16. Noelle-Neumann, *The Germans,* p. 490. Curiously, the rising optimism on behalf of German newlyweds was accompanied by a dropping marriage and birth rate. On another question as many as 5 percent (1976) and 9 percent (1979), when asked to speculate on the future, ventured the guess that "in five or ten years" a new world war may have broken out. Ibid., p. 493.

17. Given the memories of the German conquest and occupation of parts of the Soviet Union in World War II among the older generation, there may well be a link between the expectation of Soviet wrath and a "threatening" Soviet Union.

18. Merkl, "Politico-Cultural Restraints," p. 459; J. Fullenbach and E. Schulz, eds., *Entspannung am Ende?* (Munich: Oldenbourg, 1980), p. 101.

19. Noelle-Neumann, *The Germans,* p. 430. In 1968 the perception of a Soviet threat shot up to 54 percent because of the invasion of Czechoslovakia, and in 1979, before the Afghanistan crisis, it slumped to a mere 35 percent (32 percent did not feel threatened in 1968 and 46 percent in 1979). There

were no notable differences among the age groups and only mild ones between the supporters of right- and left-wing parties on this question.

20. Ibid., p. 429. When asked in 1977 whether they believed that Leonid Brezhnev "aims for peaceful cooperation with the West" or Soviet dominance over Europe, 53 percent opted for domination (23 percent did not). Ibid., p. 431. German security elites, on the other hand, seem to draw careful distinctions between the concrete security threat and an image of Soviet "aggressiveness" that fluctuates with different issues and even at different stages of ongoing negotiations, such as those over the MBFR. See Peter Schmidt and Matthias Jung in Dietmar Schoessler, ed., *Militär und Politik* (Koblenz: Bernard & Graefe, 1983), esp. Tables 8–11, which distinguish between an aggressive, offensive, and defensive image of the Soviets.

21. For the Soviet perspective on the uses of Soviet strength, see also Christoph Royens, *Die sowjetische Koexistenzpolitik gegenüber Westeuropa* (Baden-Baden: Nomos, 1978), pp. 110–117. Also Noelle-Neumann, *The Germans*, pp. 433 and 436–437. Throughout the 1970s (1971–1980) a good one-third (29–37 percent) believed that "we together with NATO" could not "defend ourselves against a serious Russian attack." A smaller percentage thought NATO had enough troops and was sufficiently well armed.

22. Noelle-Neumann, *The Germans*, p. 459. But there was also majority support for statements arguing the status quo, German self-determination, and for distrust for the East.

23. Ibid., p. 460. Even among adherents of the CDU/CSU, a plurality of 42 percent versus 34 percent accepted the Oder-Neisse border.

24. Ibid., pp. 460–461. On the ratification of the treaties see Merkl, *German Foreign Policies*, pp. 165–173.

25. Noelle-Neumann, *The Germans*, pp. 429, 458, 462, and 466. In 1976, 47 percent (versus 35 percent) expressed their misgivings about a reparations payment to Poland of DM 1.2 billion and a loan of another billion in exchange for permitting the emigration of 125,000 German ethnics.

26. Ibid., pp. 477 and 466. Again, age differences make little difference in the support for continuing détente although the supporters of the government parties SPD-FDP were more heavily for it (89 percent and 85 percent respectively) than CDU/CSU adherents (59 percent vs. 28 percent). This positive attitude toward détente continued despite, or perhaps because of, the different wind blowing from Washington. In late 1983 a Sinus Institute study ascertained a level of 87 percent in support of continuing détente. *Sicherheitspolitik, Bündnispolitik, Friedensbewegung. Eine Untersuchung zur aktuellen politischen Stimmungslage im Spätherbst 1983* (Bonn: Friedrich-Ebert-Stiftung, Oct. 1983).

27. See also the evidence cited from polls and elite studies in Great Britain, the Netherlands, and the United States on the continued preference for détente (there was less support for it in France). John E. Reilly, ed., *American Public Opinion and U.S. Foreign Policy* (Chicago: Council on Foreign Relations, 1983), pp. 14–15.

28. Noelle-Neumann, *The Germans*, p. 436. See also David Gress, *Peace and Survival in West Germany, the Peace Movement and European Security* (Stanford: Hoover Institution Press, 1985), Chapters 4 and 9.

29. Noelle-Neumann, *The Germans,* p. 437.

30. Ibid., p. 426. Twenty-two percent said they did not like him personally but only 17 percent took a dim view of his policies for Germany. It should be noted that President Carter did not do much better after his election in 1976: Forty percent found him likeable (22 percent did not) but only 24 percent thought he was "good for Germany." Ibid., p. 423.

31. Ibid., pp. 420–421. There may of course be the possibility of misunderstanding the informal language of interviews. See also Gebhard Schweigler, "Anti-Americanism in German Public Opinion," in Dieter Dettke, ed., *America's Image in Germany and Europe* (Washington: Friedrich-Ebert-Stiftung, March 31, 1985), pp. 8–33.

32. See Gerhard Herdegen and Elisabeth Noelle-Neumann, "Protest Howls Belied by Opinion Polls," *The German Tribune,* June 3, 1984, pp. 10–15 (translated from *Die Politische Meinung,* No. 212 [1984]).

33. Ibid., pp. 13–14. On the question of "too hard" actions, those saying "too weak" only numbered 2–6 percent while those saying "just right" declined from 45 percent in May 1981 to 18 percent in Oct./Nov. 1982 and 24 percent in June 1983.

34. Noelle-Neumann, *The Germans,* p. 420. This question, by the way, was asked again in Oct. 1984 and received a more heartening reply: At that time 55 percent were confident and 44 percent not. Cited in Schweigler, "Anti-Americanism," p. 20. Most likely, the result would have been even more flattering to U.S. leadership had the question been asked after the Reagan-Gorbachev summit of late 1985.

35. Noelle-Neumann, *The Germans,* p. 416. Although in 1954 only 20 percent (versus 66 percent) thought it possible, in 1976 it was 49 percent, in 1979, 56 percent, and in 1981, 51 percent.

36. Ibid., p. 478, and Schweigler, "Anti-Americanism," p. 21. West Germans also have reservations about the social and economic order of the U.S. as a model for their own country, which motivates some of this neutralism. See Schweigler, "Anti-Americanism," p. 17. Schweigler does not consider this an expression of anti-Americanism.

37. Emnid data cited by Schweigler, "Anti-Americanism," p. 26.

38. Herdegen and Noelle-Neumann, "Protest Howls Belied," p. 15.

39. Noelle-Neumann, *The Germans,* p. 127. The presence of U.S. troops in the Federal Republic also has become, if anything, more popular since the 1950s when as many as 51 percent (1956) and 34 percent (1957) would have regretted their leaving. Since 1965 and through 1984, majorities between 55 percent and 60 percent have said they would regret their departure and nearly as many have said that their presence maintains the peace. Ibid., p. 427.

40. Emnid data cited by Schweigler, "Anti-Americanism," p. 31. The only puzzle in Table 3.4 is that there are such large numbers who think that deployment of the new missiles made no difference either way.

41. Evidently many who were undecided on the former question had strong opinions on deterrence that may even have run athwart their division on that question.

42. See Merkl, "Politico-Cultural Restraints," pp. 456–457.
43. See also ibid., pp. 458–459.
44. This reversal of opinion or return to previous postures is not meant to deny the continued presence of substantial pacifist, unilateral, or neutralist minorities in postwar West Germany that have existed throughout the four decades since 1945.

4

Arms Control in Europe: Prospects and Problems

Jonathan Dean

This review of the problems and prospects for arms control in Europe rests on the assumption that following the Reagan-Gorbachev summit of November 1985, bilateral U.S.-Soviet arms control negotiations in Geneva will continue in a somewhat more purposeful way than heretofore. The approach of the summit motivated both countries to present revised proposals for reduction of nuclear weapons that differ in their reasoning but have some points of similarity. It remains unclear whether a fully articulated U.S.-Soviet nuclear arms agreement, complete in all details including verification, can be reached during the present Reagan administration. But the Geneva talks may proceed in somewhat more energetic form.

This is important background for the two multilateral negotiations discussed here, the East-West Conference on Disarmament in Europe (CDE) at Stockholm[1] and the NATO–Warsaw Pact force reduction talks in Vienna (in NATO terminology, the negotiations on mutual and balanced force reductions, or MBFR). The fact that General Secretary Gorbachev and President Reagan agreed at Geneva to hold a summit in 1986 and another in 1987 is the final element needed to assure the success of the Stockholm talks and to give some impetus to the MBFR talks.

It is useful to recall at the outset that the NATO–Warsaw Pact confrontation in Europe is still the largest peacetime military concen-

---

The manuscript for this chapter was completed prior to the agreement, signed September 22, 1986, of the Conference on Disarmament in Europe, which contains detailed measures to reduce the risk of surprise attack in Europe. For the provisions of the agreement see *Arms Control Today,* November 1986, pp. 20–24.

tration in history. It constitutes the greatest destructive potential ever assembled, including, according to NATO figures, more than 6 million men in active duty military forces on both sides, 40,000 tanks, 10,000 combat aircraft, and more than 2,600 large and small naval vessels on the seas bordering Europe. In addition, about 15,000 tactical and intermediate-range nuclear warheads are deployed in Europe including the western USSR, not to mention the strategic nuclear weapons aimed at targets in Europe. This huge military concentration costs about two-thirds of the world's trillion dollar annual expenditure for armed forces.

Today, the NATO–Warsaw Pact confrontation appears stable. Few leaders on either side expect aggressive attack from the other. In my own view, although there is evidence against it, the East-West military confrontation has already passed its high point, at least politically, and, however imperceptibly and unclearly, may be gradually running down. Although there is disagreement on this point also, it is possible to conceive of the Soviet Union following a status quo policy in Europe while continuing vigorous efforts to expand its influence in the Third World. If so, the resulting situation, a confrontation in decline, would have its own dangers to which we should devote serious analysis.

But it is not necessary to share this view to consider the European confrontation a dangerous one. A force confrontation of this magnitude is like a gigantic nuclear mine, sensitive to detonation by external pressures such as East-West conflict in Third World countries or widespread unrest in Eastern Europe. A confrontation of this nature and dimension also contains worrisome possibilities of human error, miscalculation, and misperception that could trigger conflict. Twice in 1984, U.S. helicopters entered Czechoslovakian territory or approached it and were reportedly fired on. This is good reason to think seriously of a NATO–Warsaw Pact risk reduction center in Europe similar to the U.S.-Soviet center under discussion.

This is also more than sufficient reason to do something about the risks and the costs of this confrontation through East-West negotiations on other security issues. True, many still believe that the confrontation has in itself kept the peace in Europe and has prevented war. They consider that it will continue to do so without the need for negotiated restrictions as long as an East-West balance is preserved, even with increased expense and destructive power. We sometimes hear the same reasoning about the U.S.-Soviet nuclear confrontation. And it is true that the huge excess of nuclear weapons in practice guarantees an assured capacity to retaliate. But this view is fatalistic to the point of irresponsibility, placing excessive reliance on human rationality. It is complacent in the belief that the present will continue unchanged into the indefinite future.

In any event, the number of those in both Europe and the United States who consider the confrontation to be unnecessarily expensive or increasingly dangerous, and who want not only negotiation but results from negotiation, seems on the increase. Negotiation is a necessary part of any effort to improve East-West political relations.

The Conference on Disarmament in Europe

Nine years of effort to continue the modest beginnings on security issues of the 1975 Helsinki Conference on Security and Cooperation in Europe (CSCE)[2] led to the CDE conference in Stockholm in January 1984; the outcome of that meeting was to be reported at the next Helsinki Review Conference in Vienna in November 1986. The reporting requirement is significant for future prospects of the Stockholm talks. Like their beginning, the progress of the Stockholm negotiations has been relatively slow. The first months were spent in presentation and justification of proposals by participants. It took nearly a year to reach agreement on procedures for more detailed examination of proposals through establishing two working groups.

The program of confidence-building measures that NATO participants proposed in January 1984 represents essentially an expansion and tightening of the Helsinki Accords provisions on pre-notification of military exercises, extending the notification criteria to cover most out-of-garrison activities and requiring longer advance notice for such activities. Three of the six Western proposals dealt directly with this topic.[3] Five of the six proposals put forward by the Soviet Union in its draft treaty of May 1984 called for general political commitments instead of the specific, rather limited Western confidence-building measures. The Soviet Union urged (1) nonuse of force by participants against each other; (2) prohibition of first use of nuclear weapons; (3) establishment of zones free of nuclear weapons; (4) mutual reduction of military budgets; and (5) a ban on chemical weapons in Europe. But, like the West, the Soviet Union proposed expansion of the Helsinki measure on pre-notification of exercises—including restrictions on the size of land maneuvers and greater precision on pre-notification of troop movements—as well as improved practices for inviting observers to maneuvers.

The NATO participants have long had in mind a compromise between these approaches, with NATO including in an agreement a commitment on nonuse of force in return for Warsaw Pact agreement to specific confidence-building measures proposed by the NATO participants. By mid-1985, Warsaw Pact participants were moving in this direction. They had ceased to press vigorously for most items of their more general program. Their ideas on formulation of a commitment not to use force, their desire to expand coverage of an agreement to air and naval exercises in the Atlantic, and their restriction of coverage of notification measures to formal maneuvers still represent important differences from the NATO positions.

Nonetheless, the essential components of a first CDE agreement appear to be already on the table. During his visit to Paris in the fall of 1985, General Secretary Gorbachev announced Soviet agreement to a central NATO concept: an annual calendar of maneuvers, representing a normal pattern of force activities, to be exchanged in advance. With the help of the November 1986 deadline and the approach of a second Reagan-Gorbachev summit, and in the absence of a flare-up in East-West relations in the intervening period, it is quite likely that the summer and fall of 1986 will see conclusion of a first CDE agreement on the nonuse of force and several of the confidence-building measures proposed by the NATO participants.

An interesting development of recent months has been the increasing support of the neutrals and nonaligned, especially Sweden, Finland, Switzerland, and Austria, for some form of inspection for compliance with agreed measures. There has also been some informal indication of Warsaw Pact willingness to discuss this possibility in return for concessions in other areas of a possible agreement, especially the issue of coverage of some air and naval maneuvers. True, what is being discussed at Stockholm is the Warsaw Treaty approach to inspections, called "challenge inspection." Under this procedure, justification of a complaint is discussed, and the country receiving the complaint decides whether an inspection is justified. This approach differs from the inspection concept that NATO states now innocuously call routine inspection and that Pact states sometimes criticize as fishing for intelligence information. Under the NATO concept, the country initiating the request for inspection can carry it out after an agreed interval and under agreed conditions, whether or not the inspected country considers the request justified. This distinction promises to become a central issue at the Vienna talks as well.

The Soviet Union, other Warsaw Treaty participants, and the neutral and nonaligned are pressing in Stockholm for agreement to limit the size of out-of-garrison activities. Some NATO members support the concept, but not overtly in the negotiations. The United States has been cool to this idea, partly because of its general unwillingness to have any such constraints included in a first CDE agreement and partly because limitation of the size of maneuvers at the level needed to permit continuation of NATO combined exercises of the present large scope would stop almost no current Pact exercises.

Nonetheless, this approach does have clear benefits for inhibiting large force concentrations and for early warning of unannounced concentrations. If ultimately it is supported not only by the Soviet Union and the neutrals but also by the Federal Republic, this will represent a key grouping for the dynamics of this multilateral conference at Stockholm: When the Soviets agree, most other Warsaw Pact members fall into line; and when the Federal Republic agrees, other European NATO countries usually ultimately agree. Faced by this combination, the United States usually goes along too. Given these facts of decisionmaking at CDE, a measure restricting the size of out-of-garrison maneuvers may be included in a first agreement.

Assuming agreement in Stockholm on the basis described here, what would be the military significance of a first CDE agreement and its implications for the future? This first CDE agreement would contain no reductions, no limitations on the size of forces, and, at best, only limited restrictions on military activities. It would make no direct contribution to damping down the NATO–Warsaw Pact arms race: The competition in modernized armaments would remain wholly unrestricted. The great success of the Madrid Review Conference has been in obtaining Soviet agreement to expand the area of application of the CDE conference to include the Soviet Union west of the Urals. But this advance is at the same time the greatest weakness of the CDE format: If one thinks in very long periods of time, perhaps this obstacle is surmountable. But, for the foreseeable future, it seems unlikely that the Soviet Union would agree to reductions and limitations of Soviet forces on its own territory.

Moreover, present Western proposals at Stockholm suspend the requirement for pre-notification and for inviting observers in the initial stages of alerts and mobilization exercises. Additional exceptions will be requested for U.S. troops in transit from other areas via Europe to third areas. All these exceptions would create a big loophole in the coverage of these measures. A good deal of preparation for surprise attack could take place during one of these unannounced alerts even though the time period for suspension of coverage may be limited to thirty-six hours or so. The potential damage could be limited if the maximum size of alerts were limited.

The greatest benefit of such a first-phase CDE would be political, demonstrating that East and West can reach agreement. The second major benefit would be in opening the door to a second phase of CDE with a more serious content. It has not been decided whether there will be a second phase of CDE or what its mandate would be, but we can assume with some certainty that a second phase will come about and also that it will be followed by other phases.

The Mutual and Balanced Force Reduction Talks

In theory, the MBFR talks in Vienna hold more promise than does CDE of seriously contributing to managing the East-West military confrontation in Europe. MBFR's alliance-to-alliance format assures the participation of those states directly involved in the European confrontation. Regrettably, France still declines to participate, but the Vienna force reduction talks benefit from the absence of erratic elements like Malta, whose insistence on discussion of its impractical, far-reaching proposals has added a great deal of time to discussion of security issues in the CSCE framework. As is widely known, for eight years the Vienna talks have been held up by the dispute between NATO and Pact participants over the number of active duty Warsaw Pact ground and air force personnel in Central Europe. NATO has in the past estimated the total number of these personnel at 220,000 more than the figures presented by the Warsaw Pact for their own ground forces. As I and others have been urging for some time, the current NATO requirement for prior agreement on data should be suspended so that a limited first U.S.-Soviet reduction can be agreed upon; the data dispute should then be resolved on-site through inspections rather than at the negotiating table.

While controversy over data has dragged on, agreement in principle has been reached in Vienna on many components of a first MBFR agreement, including goals and structure[4] as well as associated measures designed to verify residual ceilings and provide assurance against surprise attack.[5] The measures include agreement in principle on inspections by forces of the opposing alliance, a most important item. The best way to check the levels of military manpower in a large area is probably by sampling inspections of arbitrarily selected Soviet and Pact units on the basis of figures for the inspected units supplied by their governments. To bring this about, NATO countries participating in the Vienna talks will have to do what they should have done long ago—engage Warsaw Pact countries in a systematic discussion of the practical details of inspections and seek to convert their agreement to inspections (in principle) into a workable inspection regime. It is difficult to understand why NATO countries like the United States, which so strongly stress verification, have so long neglected this opportunity to explore with the Soviet Union and other Pact members the possibility of on-site inspection and to test their willingness to agree to workable verification. In any event, thinking in Allied capitals appears to be moving in this direction, raising the prospect that the Vienna talks will again become businesslike. At least this could become a real test of Soviet willingness to accept inspections.

Thus, a first agreement in MBFR with a modest reduction of U.S. and Soviet forces is a possibility. Again, the major importance of such an agreement would be political: It would demonstrate that, after nearly forty years of military confrontation, East and West can agree on measures to reduce the confrontation. This demonstration would be valuable in itself, however modest the outcome: It would be inappropriate to apply purely military standards of gains or losses to agreements whose military significance has deliberately been kept limited by decisionmakers on both sides.

However, some military benefits would result. A first agreement on this basis would lead to withdrawal of two Soviet divisions from Central Europe, freeze remaining Warsaw Pact military personnel at its present level, and institute a regime of verification, advance notification, and observation and inspection that would markedly reduce the possibility of surprise attack by either alliance.

The Costs of Possible Success

We must acknowledge that even if both the CDE and MBFR conferences culminate in a first agreement not a great deal will have been done either to reduce the size, risks, or costs of the existing military confrontation or even to devise better means of managing it. And there are many other problems for the future. First, there is concern in many quarters in the United States, and in Europe too, about the political impact of such agreements on the defense morale of the Western public—its willingness to continue paying the higher costs of defense. The political costs of *not* reaching agreement on some specific measures of arms control in Europe will probably be even more serious for European defense morale than the effects of modest first agreements, though skeptics are not convinced.

Second, the main obstacle to a more ambitious approach to force reductions in Europe is the Soviet interest in maintaining the military status quo, at least as far as conventional forces are concerned. It is almost certain that the Soviet Union will continue to insist on keeping large forces in forward positions in Eastern Europe, primarily because they are required to prop up the governments of Eastern Europe. Soviet leaders are unlikely to admit this motivation to themselves or to review dispassionately how many forces are needed for purposes of political control. Such candor has to await radical change in the Soviet system, of which there is no sign whatever. It is improbable that these Soviet forces will be used to attack Western Europe, but neither will they be moved back.

Powerful institutional interests will continue to support this essentially political motivation for keeping Soviet troops in Central Europe at much their present level. The main *raison d'être* of the Soviet ground forces and of their own claim on important allocations of Soviet resources is to deal with the Western military threat as they perceive and present it to the Soviet leadership. This means in practical terms that the Soviet Union will not only insist that large Soviet forces remain in Eastern Europe but that these forces be well equipped—requiring a balancing NATO force. In a sense, we will all keep on paying in this way for the inadequacies off the Soviet system. For the foreseeable future, these factors appear to limit the possible scope of reductions of Soviet forces in Eastern Europe. If this reasoning is correct—and the Soviets are not willing to make large reductions in their forces but still have some interest in moving toward decreasing the risks of confrontation—we may have to think of ways to restructure Warsaw Treaty and NATO forces through zones of prohibited armament and similar devices.

There are many additional military problems for further MBFR agreements. First, military staffs in NATO countries feel that they may not be able to afford further force reductions in the somewhat changed circumstances since the outset of the Vienna talks. Second, there is the continuing general argument about the significance for Western military security of reductions and limitations of armed forces. Responding to this argument, we must ask to what extent even modest improvement in East-West political relations in Europe is feasible while Soviet and Warsaw Pact forces that could be used in a conflict in Europe continue to outnumber Western European forces and to undergo continual modernization with new and better equipment. Third, dispute continues over the military significance of Soviet reductions if these reductions involve only withdrawal to the territory of the USSR. On this last point, the benefits of Soviet withdrawals are evident if, as has already occurred, Soviet forces withdrawn to the Soviet Union are converted to low-readiness reserve status. The resulting gain in warning time that would permit mobilization of European reserves and arrival in Europe of U.S. reinforcements in the three to four weeks needed to bring these Soviet units to combat readiness may lead to a possible amendment of the Western program in future phases of MBFR.

The second phase of CDE, as I see it, should consist mainly of further constraints on troop activities—limitations on the size, duration, frequency, and location of out-of-garrison activities, possibly on their nature, what they can exercise—and on what equipment they can use. These restrictions would be worthwhile but would involve further problems because it is unlikely that military commands on either side will be happy with them. The level of military toleration for measures with a real bite is quite low. Even when restrictions have at least equal effect on both sides, the traditional military reaction, both in Europe and in the U.S.-Soviet strategic relationship, is to prefer one's own flexibility of action over contractual restraints on the potential adversary.

Further problems would arise from the relationships between MBFR and CDE if agreement is reached in both forums or even if there is agreement in CDE but not MBFR. Many of the obligations now foreseen are overlapping, and confusion could result if agreement were reached in both conferences. A related problem is the preference of the Federal Republic for the much larger CDE area from the Atlantic to the Urals, which includes the western USSR as well as France and the United Kingdom, as compared to the smaller Central European MBFR reduction area.[6] This preference is motivated in part by a desire to avoid controls and restrictions to which the Federal Republic's European allies would not be subject, as well as a desire to apply these restrictions to Soviet forces in the western USSR that would be used in a conflict in Europe. The Federal Republic may be led to support a fusion of the MBFR and CDE negotiations. Given Soviet resistance to applying restrictions on their forces in the USSR, this amalgamation might have to be made at the cost of closing off the possibility of further reductions and limitations of NATO and Pact forces for some years to come. A theoretical solution might be found if France were willing to open its territory for reductions in the CDE context in return for Soviet action to do the same for that portion of its territory covered by the CDE. France might be willing, but Soviet willingness to do this is improbable.

From the U.S. viewpoint, among the most serious problems of arms control in Europe is Western European, especially West German, ambivalence on this general subject. West German opinion strongly supports negotiation on arms control issues affecting Europe, but, like U.S. opinion on strategic arms control, West German opinion is sharply divided over the desirability of actually concluding arms control agreements with the Soviet Union and over the compromises necessary to achieve actual agreement. The past decade has shown that U.S. political leaders tend to take a detached view of arms control in Europe, leaving it up to Western European NATO members to provide the impetus for such endeavors. As noted, the United States usually goes along, however reluctantly, in cases (such as CDE) in which Western Europe and the Soviet Union have reached agreement on particular measures. And here the Federal Republic plays a key role, but where German opinion is not agreed—as in the case of the useful MBFR proposal that no individual national force should have more than 50 percent of the total strength of its alliance—nothing has happened, and this will continue to be the case in the future as well. When there is no movement in one or the other negotiation, the resulting frustration and blame, which sometimes actually reflects lack of consensus in the Federal Republic, is often directed at the United States.

For example, we would be far better off today in the still unresolved negotiation over INF missiles if both Social Democrats and Christian Democrats had been able to act together in support of the "walk in the woods" compromise, which leaders of both parties subsequently and separately welcomed. Even given the wide differences of opinion and the need to present the electorate with clear alternatives, West German government and opposition should still be able to agree on specific arms control issues in order to make the German contribution more effective than it often has been—to the benefit of all.

Another potentially serious problem is already emerging. Unless the Geneva negotiations are successful in working out some *modus vivendi* on ballistic missile defense, increasing controversy in Europe and between the United States and Europe over missile defense and its effects on arms control is probable. If so, pressures for unilateral Western measures of arms reduction in Europe are likely to intensify. Beyond that, the issue of defense against tactical ballistic missiles is likely to become the focus of controversy in Europe. Here, the same rule applies as in defense against strategic missiles: Defense will not work unless the offense is limited by agreement, and offensive systems cannot be effectively limited by agreement unless defensive systems are limited also. Sooner or later, there will have to be East-West discussion of both of these topics in some forum, preferably one with direct European participation, as should be the case in Geneva today. This point draws attention to other omissions in the scope of existing arms control negotiation in Europe. There are no negotiations now over reduction of armaments in the area of tactical nuclear weapons, chemical weapons, or tanks, and no negotiations on limitation of qualitative improvements in armaments such as exist (however inadequately) for anti-ballistic missile defense.

Most NATO governments are aware of these and other problems, but have been content to let them continue. Taken together, these issues and problems mean intellectual disorder, lack of goals, and the absence of an integrating concept in the whole field of European arms control. But these governments are now faced with possible success of the negotiations and must get serious about the unresolved problems of arms control in Europe. It is possible that the MBFR talks will have a positive outcome within a year, and it is probable that the CDE will. Already it is clear that if one or both negotiations succeed, they will continue in some form. There is need now for systematic thinking about the desired future direction of arms control in Europe. Do we want reduction of armaments in Central Europe if Soviet forces in the western

USSR are not reduced? If not, what can we do to bring the Soviets to accept arms control on their own territory? Can this problem be solved by requiring withdrawn Soviet units to be placed on reserve status? (This status could be checked by national technical means and would be easier to negotiate than a complete regime of reductions and limitations on Soviet territory.) Is it really true that the Soviets will resist significant reductions in Eastern Europe? Is the idea of reductions and limitations so discredited in general that it should be relinquished in favor of restructuring and restricting location of units and armaments? If so, how should it be done?

During the next year the United States and the countries of Europe should try to move toward some overall concept that would combine answers to these questions in an integrated long-range plan. In practical terms, the process has to start in Europe and should then be taken up with the U.S. administration. It might prove useful to conduct an informal exploratory discussion with Warsaw Pact representatives (perhaps in Vienna, parallel to the MBFR talks) to exchange general ideas before the next phase starts. The effort to develop an integrated long-range plan in the West for arms control in Europe may not succeed, but the effort to conceive one will probably shed light on individual arms control steps that could be taken in the future.

Notes

1. The Conference on Confidence- and Security-Building Measures and Disarmament in Europe, which began in January 1984, included the thirty-five signatory states of the 1975 Helsinki Accords. The full title is cumbersome; most treatments of the subject in English use the term "Conference on Disarmament in Europe," or CDE.

2. The Helsinki Final Act provided that signatories would notify each other twenty-one days in advance of military maneuvers exceeding a total of 25,000 troops taking place in an area extending from the Atlantic coast through a 250-km strip of the Soviet Union along its western border. Participants could also at their own option invite observers from other signatory states to these maneuvers and could give advance notification of smaller maneuvers.

3. The NATO proposals are (1) exchange of information among participants on their military forces, providing unit designation, location, and strength of units down to brigade or regiment level; (2) exchange of annual forecasts of military activities, including exercises and other out-of-garrison movements, at a threshold of 6,000 men or of a combiantion of units composing the combat elements of a division; (3) specific notification, forty-five days in advance, of all out-of-garrison activities of forces of the dimensions just described; (4) a requirement that states invite observers to out-of-garrison activities; (5) verification, consisting of noninterference with national technical means and a limited

number of inspections per year on the territory in Europe of participants to test compliance with the other confidence-building measures; and (6) improved communications, military exchanges, hot lines, and so on, to be worked out and agreed upon among conference participants on a bilateral basis.

4. The points include (1) agreement on the long-term goal of reducing ground force personnel in the Central European reduction area to a ceiling of 700,000 for both alliances, with a combined common ceiling of 900,000 for the total ground and air force personnel of each alliance; (2) initial reductions of U.S. and Soviet personnel in the general range of 10,000 to 30,000 respectively; (3) a residual ceiling on Soviet and U.S. ground force personnel and a freeze on the remaining personnel of each alliance; and (4) further reductions by all participants.

5. In addition to inspections, the measures include (1) pre-notification of entry into the area of larger numbers of personnel (20,000–25,000); (2) use of exit-entry points manned by military personnel of the other side for those entering or leaving the area; (3) pre-notification of out-of-garrison activity of division-size forces (the presence of observers at these movements has not yet been agreed); (4) exchange of information on forces remaining in the area following reductions (the scope of such exchange remains to be agreed); and (5) a consultative process.

6. The MBFR reduction area consists of the territory of Benelux and the Federal Republic of Germany on the Western side and of the GDR, Poland, and Czechoslovakia on the Eastern side.

5

Extended Deterrence, No First Use, and European Security

John P. Holdren

Introduction

Extended deterrence "extends" in two dimensions: (1) to cover threats to one's allies as well as to one's own country and (2) to cover nonnuclear as well as nuclear threats. I am most interested here in the second of these dimensions—that is, in the concept that threatening to use nuclear weapons in response to a conventional attack is a legitimate and effective means of deterring such attacks. In the case of NATO policy both forms of extension are involved, but the second dimension is the most troublesome. The U.S. commitment to respond with nuclear weapons to *nuclear* attacks on its NATO allies is not nearly as fragile, as controversial, or as dangerous as the commitment to respond with nuclear weapons to a *conventional* attack.

Historically the extended form of nuclear deterrence preceded the narrower form: U.S. possession of nuclear weapons was widely believed to offer protection to Western Europe against the powerful conventional forces of the Soviet Union in the immediate aftermath of World War II—when there were no Soviet nuclear weapons (Herken, 1981). The NATO alliance itself, only a few months old when the Soviet Union exploded its first nuclear bomb in August 1949, was doubtless discomfited by that event; but it was not deflected from its conviction that U.S. nuclear weapons could and should compensate for the alliance's inability or unwillingness to field larger conventional forces—regardless of the further deterrent burdens that might be imposed on U.S. nuclear forces by Soviet possession of the same types of weapons.

NATO has managed to cling to that conviction for decades, but the stresses and strains of doing so have been great. Indeed, the most difficult and divisive internal controversies in the history of the alliance—the abortive attempt in the early 1960s to create within NATO a nuclear multilateral force (MLF), the withdrawal of France from the military structure of the alliance in the mid-1960s, the neutron bomb debate of the mid-1970s, the Pershing II and GLCM deployments following NATO's double-track decision of December 1979, and the recurrent debates about the relative contributions of the United States and its European allies to the collective defense—all have been entangled to a greater or lesser degree with the issue of extended deterrence. (For a variety of perspectives on this history, see Hoffman, 1979, 1983; Freedman, 1981; Joffe, 1983; Schwartz, 1983.)

At the core of the question of nuclear deterrence of conventional threats is NATO's long-standing declaratory policy of "first use of nuclear weapons if necessary" together with its consequences for military procurements, force postures, contingency plans, adversary perceptions, and, ultimately, for the probabilities of conventional and nuclear conflict. This set of issues was given new prominence in public debate by the publication of an article by McGeorge Bundy, George Kennan, Robert McNamara, and Gerard Smith arguing that NATO should move toward a policy and posture of no first use and by an ensuing flood of responses and expanded analyses. (Among the latter see especially Kaiser et al., 1982; Union of Concerned Scientists, 1983; Steinbruner and Sigal, 1983; European Security Study, 1983; Blackaby et al., 1984; Lee, 1984; Mearsheimer, 1984/85.)

Without pretending to offer a comprehensive review of the rich history of this debate and of the diverse contentions that have recently been put forward on all sides, I offer a relatively brief attempt in three parts to get to the heart of the issue: first, a critique of NATO's policy of extended deterrence on the grounds that it makes our biggest problems bigger while seeking to make our smallest problems smaller; second, a brief listing and comparison of the alternatives to the present policy; and third, a response to criticisms that a NATO no-first-use declaration would be intolerably dangerous at worst and meaningless at best.

A Critique of Extended Deterrence

In theory, the threat to use nuclear weapons against a conventional attack can contribute to deterring such an attack in two ways. First, the potential attacker may fear that the defender's use of nuclear weapons would be a militarily effective response to the attack. The attacker is deterred by the prospect of denial of the attack's objectives. Second, the potential aggressor may fear that any use of nuclear forces would be so likely to escalate to the regional and then to the global scale that attacking an adversary armed with nuclear weapons entails too great a risk of ultimate catastrophe. The aggressor is deterred by the prospect of punishment.

For deterrence of the first sort to be effective, the defender must be able to use nuclear weapons in ways that deny the attacker's objectives without at the same time destroying what is being defended. This notion has underpinned the development of nuclear artillery, nuclear land mines, short-range nuclear missiles, and, most recently, the neutron bomb. Alas, these developments all have been in vain. In the first place, the use of nuclear weapons on the battlefield offers no particular military advantage to the defending side when the offense also possesses such weapons in abundance: A battle being lost with conventional weapons probably will be lost even more rapidly if both sides are using battlefield nuclear weapons (Carver, 1982; Bundy et al., 1982; McNamara, 1983). Secondly, the "collateral" damage to civilian populations and property associated with the use even of "small" nuclear weapons would be staggering, a problem made all the more serious for NATO by the fact that short-range nuclear weapons used against a Warsaw Pact invasion that had overrun NATO's conventional defenses would be exploding deep in NATO's own territory.

There is no doubt that use of battlefield and theater nuclear weapons on a very large scale—as opposed to limited battlefield use—could bring a conventional attack to a halt and indeed make it irrelevant. The trouble is that this goal would be accomplished only at the cost of wholesale destruction of the very territory and society being defended (Zuckerman, 1982; Bundy et al., 1982). Even if the result did not include the escalation of nuclear warfare to a global scale, such an outcome could hardly be considered a military victory. Contemplation of the results of large-scale use of nuclear weapons on European battlefields, in fact, should deter NATO from carrying out such use at least as much as its possibility deters the Soviets from attacking in the first place. (This phenomenon is sometimes termed "self-deterrence.") In short, the idea that NATO's use of nuclear weapons—whether on a modest scale or in much larger numbers—would be militarily effective against a Soviet conventional attack is too implausible to have much deterrent value.

The second way the threat to introduce nuclear weapons might deter conventional aggression is through the potential aggressor's fear that any use of nuclear forces would be likely to escalate not only to the regional but also to the global scale, thus destroying not just the contested region but the aggressor's homeland as well. Unquestionably, a degree of extended deterrence of this sort is created simply by virtue of the existence of long-range nuclear weapons: No special policy is required to make plain that any large-scale conflict involving the central interests of the possessors of such weapons conceivably could lead to their use.

But the policy of extended deterrence has sought deliberately to make escalation to regional and global use seem more likely—more "credible"—than it would otherwise be, and herein lies great danger.

Problems of Credibility

For the first two decades of NATO's extended-deterrence policy—from the inception of NATO in 1949 until about 1970—the credibility of the threat to use nuclear weapons against a conventional attack was thought to depend on the superiority of NATO's nuclear forces over those of the Soviet Union, not simply in battlefield nuclear weapons but also in the longer-range theater and intercontinental categories. Such superiority was said to provide "escalation dominance" for NATO: At each possible level of hostilities short of global nuclear war—conventional conflict, battlefield use of nuclear weapons, regional nuclear war—NATO would have a credible option to escalate to the next level because of its superiority on that level (Freedman, 1981; Rosenberg, 1983). The prospect of escalation, in other words, would threaten the Soviets more than it threatened NATO.

This, at least, was the rationale. In reality, the concept of escalation dominance was outmoded long before this fact was generally recognized. Given the enormous destructiveness of nuclear weapons, the Soviet Union did not need numerical equality with NATO's (mostly U.S.) nuclear forces in order to be able to inflict intolerable destruction at the regional or intercontinental level. Deliberate escalation had ceased to be a rational option for NATO by the early 1960s, perhaps earlier. Escalation might well occur through accidents, mistakes, or irrational decisions—and fear of such possibilities would continue to provide de facto extended deterrence—but surely there could not be much additional deterrent value in a policy that pretended, against all evidence, that escalation was rational.

Still, NATO clung to its policy of extended deterrence—and clings to it today. By the mid-1970s, Soviet achievement of essential equivalence with NATO in battlefield, theater, and strategic nuclear weapons had made the irrationality of an explicit policy of escalation so obvious that prominent political figures began to speak publilcly of the need to restore "credibility" to NATO's posture (see, for example, Olive and Porro, 1983; Krell et al., 1983). The most noteworthy single example, of course, was Chancellor Helmut Schmidt's 1977 lecture at the International Institute of Strategic Studies. NATO's response to this predicament, far from changing its declared policy, was to continue to deploy nuclear forces whose characteristics make it plausible that escalation will be automatic even if it is irrational (Ball, 1981).

For example, nuclear artillery (upgraded versions of which are being pursued by the Pentagon even now) promotes automatic escalation from the conventional level because its short range necessitates deploying it near the front, where the pressures to use it will be intense. There is, moreover, a strong incentive for NATO to use nuclear artillery and other short-range nuclear weapons early in a conflict if they are to be used at all, because the longer one waits the deeper in one's own territory the nuclear explosions will take place (assuming that the rationale for resorting to nuclear weapons is indeed that the conventional conflict is being lost). The incentives and pressures to use short-range nuclear weapons early, coupled with a time requirement often estimated at about twenty-four hours for a field officer's request for permission to use nuclear weapons to be transmitted up the chain of command and a response to be transmitted back down, may well produce requests for pre-delegation of such authority even before a real need is perceived.

Indeed, the integration of nuclear with conventional forces at every level of organization (from that of long-range strike forces to that of short-range artillery) entails a degree of "nuclearization" of military thinking and planning that itself strongly contributes to the prospect of almost any conventional conflict in Europe quickly becoming nuclear. Vice Admiral (ret.) John Marshall Lee has described this phenomenon:

> The overriding defect of nuclear deterrence of conventional hostilities is that it irresistibly nuclearizes the national strategies, the armed forces, and the national security apparatus. With it, nuclear use is always the dominant military consideration. Military education and training, military hardware, plans, deployments, operations—the whole military/security machinery—are based on the concept that nuclear weapons may be brought into conventional operations at any time. Nuclear capabilities are brought into nearly all elements of the armed forces; nuclear operations are trained for; nuclear readiness is kept high. Military commanders will expect nuclear support when it appears necessary on nuclear grounds; they will call for it when in difficulties. National leaders, under appalling stresses, in the fog of war, receiving drumfire of demands for nuclear operations, conditioned like the military to nuclear use, will be under enormous pressure to issue the nuclear release. (Lee, 1984)

The thorough integration of nuclear and conventional forces and planning also contributes to the likelihood of early resort to nuclear weapons in another way: The resources that field commanders must devote to the protection, husbanding, and management of their nuclear weapons and associated delivery capabilities represent reduction in their capabilities to carry out their assigned missions conventionally (Sigal, 1983a; Lee, 1984).

Once the conventional-nuclear "firebreak" has been breached at the battlefield level, moreover, the pressure to use the medium-range or theater nuclear forces will become intense, largely because the combination of accuracy and vulnerability of the weapons in this category on both sides puts a premium on preemption—trying to destroy your adversary's weapons before the adversary uses them to destroy yours. Finally, the introduction by both sides of formidable long-range theater nuclear weapons—the Backfire bomber and SS-20 missile on the Soviet side, the F-111 and Tornado attack aircraft and the GLCMs and Pershing II ballistic missiles on the NATO side—has blurred the distinction between theater and strategic weapons in ways that increase the likelihood of further escalation. Indeed, in the case of the Pershing II and GLCM deployments, the "coupling" of theater and strategic forces was an explicit part of NATO's rationale; these deployments were to help convince the Soviets that a nuclear war could not be confined to Europe (Burt, 1983).

The Threat of First Use

The fundamental mistake behind NATO's continuing reliance on an explicit policy of "first use of nuclear weapons if necessary" is the failure to distinguish between two types of threat to peace, one of them quite susceptible to reduction by deterrence and the other hardly susceptible at all. The first type is the threat of premeditated attack by a rational aggressor who calculates that the expected gain from aggression outweighs the expected costs and risks. The risk that such aggression will lead to the use of nuclear weapons and to escalation toward global nuclear conflict is a powerful deterrent against this type of threat. The second type is the threat of conflict initiated by preemptive pressures during a crisis, by accident or mistake during the hair-trigger circumstances that a crisis would create, or by the crazed act of a wholly irrational individual or group. Deterrence by means of increasing the apparent risks of conflict is completely ineffective against most of the threats in this class. Against the particularly important threat associated with preemptive pressures, moreover, deterrence is only effective insofar as it is achieved with forces (nuclear or conventional), the characteristics of which provide no relative advantage to the side that strikes first.

With respect to the first class of threat—a premeditated attack by a rational aggressor—as it relates to Europe (and to other arenas where the central interests of the United States and the Soviet Union intersect), the chance of such an attack would be very low even if nuclear weapons miraculously disapeared from the calculus altogether because the expected costs and risks would still outweigh the possible gains (see, for example, Mearsheimer, 1982; Lambeth, 1982/83). Moreover, the mere existence of nuclear weapons on both sides, carrying an implicit risk that a major conventional conflict would lead to their use, is a powerful additional deterrent. Accordingly, there is very little threat left to be diminished by the incremental deterrent value of an explicit policy of extended deterrence and the deployment of nuclear forces intended to back it up.

On the other hand, the threat that conflict will occur as the result of preemptive pressures during a crisis or through accidents/mistakes or by wholly irrational acts is more plausible to begin with and is much less susceptible to diminution by deterrence. Quite the contrary, the kinds of nuclear forces engendered by the policy of extended deterrence have *increased* the chance that a nuclear conflict will start by one of these avenues, as well as the chance that a conventional conflict started in one of these ways will escalate automatically toward global nuclear war (Zuckerman, 1982; Ball, 1981). NATO's attempt to reduce a threat that already was very small—the threat of rational, premeditated aggression—has aggravated a much more dangerous class of hazards.

As if that were not enough, NATO's continuing pursuit of a nuclear-force posture that would make deliberate nuclear escalation seem more rational and hence more credible—a fundamentally impossible task— has diverted attention and money from NATO's conventional forces. Although these forces are by no means as weak as is often alleged in official analyses (compare DOD, 1985; IISS, 1984; see also Mako, 1983; Mearsheimer, 1982, 1983; Kaufman, 1983b), it is certainly possible to envision improvements that would increase their ability to contain quickly, without escalation to the nuclear level, any conventional conflict that an irrational act or other unforeseeable circumstance might produce (Boston Study Group, 1979; Fallows, 1981). Such improvements are unlikely, however, as long as overreliance on nuclear deterrence of conventional threats continues to distort NATO priorities and procurement.

It should be obvious, finally, that NATO's reserving the right to threaten the use of nuclear weapons to deter conventional aggression cannot fail to increase the legitimacy of such a posture in the eyes of other countries that feel threatened by the conventional forces of a powerful neighbor. In other words, if it is legitimate for NATO to rely on nuclear weapons for its security against a Soviet conventional attack, why is it not legitimate for Israel, Pakistan, India, Argentina, Taiwan, and others to deter powerful neighbors in the same way? Is this the approach we wish to encourage?

Alternatives to the Status Quo

I have argued above that NATO's policy of "first use of nuclear weapons if necessary" poses costs and dangers disproportionate to its modest contribution to an already strong deterrence. Only three alternatives to this status quo have possible merit: (1) Retain the policy but try to implement changes in force structure and war plans designed to reduce the chance that nuclear weapons actually would be used (a posture sometimes described as "no *early* first use"); (2) abandon the policy—that is, stop planning to use nuclear weapons first—and make corresponding changes in force postures and contingency plans, but do not announce the policy change; and (3) abandon the policy, make the corresponding changes, and announce it. (A theoretical fourth alternative—declaring a posture of no first use without taking it seriously—is too implausible to merit analytical attention.)

The first alternative would be better than no change at all (see, for example, Rogers, 1982, and Kaufmann, 1983a, for the case for this option), but it is an inadequate response to the dangers posed by continuing to threaten nuclear responses to conventional attacks. Continuing reliance on the nuclear threat would maintain the pressure to deploy nuclear forces with characteristics designed to make this posture credible, and credibility in this instance translates into an automaticity of escalation that magnifies intolerably the risks associated with small conflicts or mistakes. Such reliance also works inevitably against taking steps that might strengthen the conventional deterrent, either because these are seen as unnecessary or because they are deemed prejudicial to Soviet conviction that an attack would produce the nuclear response they most fear. It leaves in place strong incentives for the Soviets to use their own nuclear weapons to attack NATO's nuclear forces preemptively if conventional conflict breaks out. And it perpetuates the dangerous legitimization for other countries of a declared posture threatening nuclear response against conventional attack.

The second alternative, abandoning the first-use posture and making corresponding changes in forces and planning but not announcing the doctrinal shift, might be motivated by the thought that this approach could avoid a potentially divisive public debate on the change in doctrine while at the same time retaining some of the deterrent value of Soviet uncertainty about the actual posture (Sigal, 1983b, among others, has made this case). These attractions seem modest, however, compared to the shortcomings that accompany them. Most importantly, to the extent that the Soviets believe the posture remains "first use if necessary," their incentives for a preemptive attack on NATO nuclear forces will be unabated. Second, failure to announce the change to a policy of no first use deprives NATO and the world of the benefit of NATO's setting a better example for the uses of nuclear weapons than it is doing now. Finally, if the public is unaware of the change in doctrine, it may be unwilling to support any increases in military spending that might be deemed necessary to bolster the conventional forces.

It is obvious, then, that I prefer the third alternative—a NATO declaration of a policy of no first use, accompanied by changes in force postures and planning that make the new policy both practical and credible. The needed changes would include withdrawal of battlefield nuclear weapons from forward positions, which, as Herbert York (1983) and others have pointed out, would increase NATO security whether or not the Warsaw Pact reciprocated. (This is due in part to the particularly powerful temptation to preempt that is created by forward-based weapons and in part to the short range of the battlefield weapons—they threaten the territory they are supposed to defend as much as they threaten the attacker.) Modifications of conventional force posture accompanying a no-first-use policy could include increases in ammunition stocks and pre-positioned reserve equipment to improve sustainability, installation of passive barriers in the vicinity of the inter-German border to slow down a Warsaw Pact blitzkrieg, protective shelters for tactical and theater aircraft, improved procedures for rapid mobilization and reinforcement, and improved communication lines (see, for example, Kaufman, 1983b; Mearsheimer, 1983).

Although, in my opinion, a no-first-use declaration and the concrete measures needed to make it credible would be in NATO's interests whether or not reciprocal actions on the Warsaw Pact side followed, matters clearly would be improved if at the same time the Warsaw Pact would make plain what measures it was undertaking to undergird its own 1982 declaration of no first use. Equally clearly, it would be a more attractive proposition to seek a stable balance of conventional forces in Europe at lower overall levels of troops and armaments than at higher ones, which means that real progress in the mutual and balanced force reduction negotiations that have dragged on in Vienna for more than a decade (Dean, 1983; Sharp, 1984) would be a most useful incentive (or concomitant) to a NATO no-first-use posture.

Notwithstanding the apparent attractions of a NATO no-first-use policy and posture as summarized above and elaborated elsewhere (Bundy et al., 1982; Union of Concerned Scientists, 1983; Lee, 1984), the idea that NATO should adopt such a position remains a highly controversial one. Among the main counterarguments that have been put forward by critics of the idea (see especially Rogers, 1982; Kaiser et al., 1982; Mearsheimer, 1984/85) are that a NATO no-first-use declaration, if taken seriously, would (1) increase the probability of conventional war in Europe by removing a key uncertainty from the Soviet calculus of the risks and benefits of aggression; (2) permit the Warsaw Pact to concentrate its offensive forces for breakthroughs without fear that these force concentrations would be targeted by NATO's tactical nuclear weapons; (3) generate requirements for strengthening NATO's conventional forces to a degree that would be economically unaffordable and/or politically unacceptable within NATO and might arouse unwanted fears and counterreactions in the Warsaw Pact; and (4) signal a reduction in the commitment of the United States to the security and independence of Western Europe, with potentially disastrous impacts on alliance cohesion and/or proliferation of independent nuclear weapons capabilities in Europe.

Responses to Criticisms of No First Use

Most European critics of no first use argue that *no* conventional force posture could deter conflict in Europe as effectively as does the threat of escalation to global nuclear war and that the consequences of even a conventional war in Europe with modern weapons would be so devastating that it must be prevented at all costs (Kaiser et al., 1982; Krell et al., 1983). They fear, in other words, that no first use, in the attempt to reduce the danger of nuclear war in Europe, will increase the danger of a conventional war that would not be notably less destructive. They tend to see the a priori probability of conventional war as much higher than that of nuclear war, arguing that the policy of "first use if necessary" is reducing a large danger (conventional war) by a lot at the expense of increasing a small danger (nuclear war) only a little—a good trade.

I believe this logic is flawed. First, as I have already argued above, the probability of a general conventional war in Europe would be very small even if nuclear weapons did not exist at all. Second, of the additional reduction in this probability that nuclear weapons provide, a much larger part derives from their mere existence on both sides than from NATO's declared polciy of "first use if necessary" and the arrangements designed to back it up. Third, while it is true that a general conventional war in Europe would be catastrophic, it is far from clear that all or even most conventional conflicts that are conceivable would escalate so far. Indeed, it is in part because escalation looks so much harder to control in a nuclear than in a conventional conflict that a NATO posture promising early nuclearization is a prescription for disaster: This posture may contribute somewhat to reducing the already small chance of a premeditated massive conventional attack, but it increases substantially the chance that smaller but much more probable conventional conflicts originating in any number of ways (some now foreseeable and others probably not) would escalate to general nuclear war. These considerations turn on its head the claim that the threat of first use makes a big problem much smaller while making a small one only a bit bigger.

Critics of no first use are reluctant to give up the deterrent benefit of Soviet uncertainty about whether NATO would respond to a conventional attack with nuclear weapons, but, again, they seem not to have considered how much of this uncertainty derives ultimately from the existence of nuclear weapons rather than from an explicit policy and posture of first use. Increasing Soviet uncertainty beyond the level created by the mere existence of nuclear weapons on both sides might be worthwhile if it were not too expensive, but the costs of doing so through the first-use posture are too high: They include, as argued above, the aggravation of the risks in what are already the most dangerous pathways to nuclear war and the neglect of practical options for strengthening conventional deterrence.

In the most vigorous critique of the case for no first use since the response of four distinguished Germans (Kaiser et al., 1982) to the *Foreign Affairs* article of Bundy et al. (1982), John Mearsheimer (1984/85) has given an interesting but ultimately unconvincing twist to the argument about the value of the uncertainty in a first-use posture. In arguing that a NATO declaration of no first use would leave us with "the worst of both worlds," he contends that policymakers would believe the declaration represented real protection against escalation from conventional to nuclear conflict, which would make initiation of conventional conflict more likely, while the continuing existence of nuclear weapons actually would mean they might well be used in spite of declared policies.

I believe Mearsheimer (whose cogent analyses of conventional force balances and conventional deterrence I much admire) has got this particular point exactly backward. Policymakers would *not* believe they could rely on the no-first-use declarations of their adversaries as guarantees that conventional conflict will not escalate to the nuclear level. They will recognize, as clearly as Mearsheimer and I do, that as long as nuclear weapons exist they may be used. Thus this de facto deterrence will continue to exist, as I have already argued, regardless of declared policy. But as long as each side takes seriously its own declaration as an expression of intent and makes the adjustments in deployments and force posture consistent with this intention, extremely important benefits will result: The adjustments in posture will reduce the chances that nuclear war will arise from preemptive pressures, automatic escalation, misjudgment, or accident; and the declaration of intent to move away from a posture based on the usability of nuclear weapons will have a benign effect on the nonproliferation regime and on the prospects for nuclear arms control more generally.

Somewhat less important, in my view, than the question of the contribution of a first-use posture to Soviet fear of escalation is the question of such a posture's actual tactical value. The main argument of proponents of first use is that use of nuclear weapons favors the defense because the concentrations of offensive conventional forces needed to produce a breakthrough would provide better targets for the defense's nuclear weapons than the defense's more dispersed forces would provide to the offense. This intuitively appealing conclusion does not withstand detailed analysis based on the forces and tactics available to the two sides, however, nor is it consistent with the outcomes of formal "war games," which have been publicly described (see, for example, York, 1983; Kaufmann, 1983a; Lee, 1984). Accordingly, one cannot give much weight to the idea that Nato's mere threat to resort to nuclear weapons has military value because it will dissuade the Soviets from concentrating their conventional forces. There are, in any case, many ways to use nonnuclear weapons to make things unpleasant for concentrated offensive forces (Afheldt, 1983; Alternative Defense Commission, 1983; European Security Study, 1983).

What of the argument that a NATO posture of no first use would require a buildup of NATO conventional forces that is politically and economically out of reach? This contention actually is much less potent than is commonly supposed. Its biggest weakness is that, because the contribution to deterrence of NATO's "first use if necessary" policy is small in the first place (for the reasons set forth above), the need to strengthen NATO's conventional forces in compensation for dropping that policy is modest as well.

The balance of conventional forces in Europe is not easy to evaluate definitively because the answer depends not only on numbers of troops and numbers and characteristics of tanks, artillery pieces, fighter aircraft, and so on but also on factors harder to quantify such as leadership, training, morale, and the cohesion of the respective alliances under stress (Steinbruner and Sigal, 1983; Lee, 1984). In this last respect, an enormous problem for Soviet leaders if they contemplated attacking Western Europe would be uncertainty about which way the Polish, Hungarian, Czech, and East German divisions would shoot (see, for example, Lambeth, 1982/83). All things considered, NATO's existing conventional strength is probably adequate to deter any rational Soviet leader from ordering an attack (Mearsheimer, 1982), even leaving aside the "existential" deterrent effect associated with the possibility of escalation despite declared policies of no first use. It may be prudent to seek some additional insurance—a bigger margin of safety in the form of improved conventional capabilities—but the question of how much is enough will never be answerable unambiguously.

In fact, the tendency to propose a NATO buildup of conventional forces to compensate for reduced reliance on nuclear deterrence poses dangers of its own, particularly if the proposed buildup emphasizes "deep strike" capabilities that appear more offensive than defensive. (Such capabilities have been stressed by, for example, Rogers, 1982, and the European Security Study, 1983.) After all, the "worst case assessment" and "fallacy of the last move" syndromes that have helped drive the nuclear arms race operate in the conventional arena as well, and there is no benefit and much danger in an arms race in Europe featuring advanced weapons for conventional attack. Any improvements undertaken in NATO's conventional forces therefore ought to emphasize weapons and force postures whose capabilities for defense exceed their capabilities for offense. If each side possesses conventional forces that are stronger in defense than in offense, it becomes possible for both simultaneously to enjoy a margin of safety against attack by the other—a stable situation that *cannot* develop if the offensive capabilities of each force equal or exceed its defensive capabilities (Nield, 1984).

That no first use would be a more attractive proposition if conventional forces were in balance at lower rather than at higher levels cannot be doubted. It should therefore be a further stimulus to the sluggish MBFR negotiations that a NATO policy and posture of no first use of nuclear weapons—so important to reduction of the danger of nuclear conflict—may in the end be contingent on real progress in achieving reductions of conventional forces. Although one should be reluctant to complicate negotiations that already seem bogged down, the benefits of achieving a conventional balance at lower levels by giving primacy to defensive over offensive capabilities make it worthwhile to devote more attention to this aspect of the problem.

NATO and No First Use

The problems with political acceptability of a NATO posture of no first use, which generally are deemed most severe in the Federal Republic of Germany, derive from several specific difficulties (Kaiser et al., 1982; Kaufmann, 1983b; Sigal, 1983b; Krell et al., 1983): the economic burdens of further increases in defense spending to beef up NATO's conventional posture, imposed on economies already in difficulty due to low growth and deficit spending; the unappealing prospect of further militarization of the territory of the Federal Republic, which already must live with the greatest concentration of military forces of any area its size in the world; the possible need to extend the period of compulsory military service in the FRG in order to maintain personnel levels in the face of a declining population in the eligible age classes (in the United Kingdom and the United States the declining population could even force the reintroduction of conscription); and the perception that a NATO posture of no first use would represent a reduction of the commitment of the

United States to maintain the security and independence of its European allies.

These problems are real. They should not be underestimated. But it is far from clear that they are insuperable. The first three problems listed—increased economic burdens of defense, increased militarization of German (and other European) territory, and extension or expansion of compulsory military service—all could be alleviated or avoided if the MBFR negotiations produce an agreement establishing a conventional balance at lower levels. And, even without such an agreement, it may be possible to find efficiencies in a more defensively oriented posture that would permit more protection without increases in spending or militarization. Finally, even lacking that, it is not obvious that Europeans really will find the costs of an expanded conventional defense intolerable—if compared with the (increasingly obvious) risks of the "first use if necessary" status quo.

The fourth problem—the idea that a transition to a posture of no first use might be seen as a U.S. retreat from its commitment to Europe—is also not insoluble. If the new posture entails increases in U.S. military spending for the defense of Europe, as it might, this will counter any impression that the change in posture represents a retreat. If, on the other hand, the no-first-use posture is undertaken in combination with an agreement on a conventional balance at less threatening levels, this circumstance itself presumably will reassure Europeans somewhat about the dangers facing them and diminish concerns about abandonment by the United States.

It does not make much sense, in any case, for Europeans to insist that the United States government demonstrate its continuing commitment to their safety by clinging to a policy of "first use of nuclear weapons if necessary" that actually decreases the security of Europeans and Americans alike. Indeed, such insistence cannot help but hinder, in the long run, a cooperative approach to the security of the members of the NATO alliance based on constant and critical review of the nature of the threat and the practicality and effectiveness of alternative responses. Amidst the military and political realities of the 1980s, NATO's first-use posture is an anachronism that does far more harm than good.

References

Afheldt, Horst. 1983. "The Necessity, Preconditions, and Consequences of a No-First-Use Policy." In *No-First-Use*, Frank Blackaby, Jozef Goldblat, and Sverre Lodgaard, eds. London: Taylor and Francis. Pp. 57–66.

Alternative Defense Commission. 1983. *Defense Without the Bomb*. London: Taylor and Francis. See especially Chapter 5.

Ball, Desmond. 1981. "Can Nuclear War Be Controlled?" Adelphi Paper 169. London: International Institute for Strategic Studies.
Blackaby, Frank, Jozef Goldblat, and Sverre Lodgaard, eds. 1984. *No-First-Use*. London: Taylor and Francis.
Boston Study Group. 1979. *The Price of Defense: A New Strategy for Military Spending*. New York: Times Books.
Bundy, McGeorge, George F. Kennan, Robert S. McNamara, and Gerard Smith. 1982. "Nuclear Weapons and the Atlantic Alliance." *Foreign Affairs*, vol. 60, no. 4 (Spring): 753–768.
Burt, Richard. 1983. "NATO and Nuclear Deterrence." In *Nuclear Weapons in Europe*, Marsha McGraw Olive and Jeffrey Porro, eds. Lexington, Mass.: Lexington Books. Pp. 109–119.
Carver, Field Marshal Lord Michael. 1982. *A Policy for Peace*. London: Faber and Faber.
Dean, Jonathan. 1983. "MBFR: From Apathy to Accord." *International Security*, vol. 7, no. 4 (Spring): 116–139.
DOD (U.S. Department of Defense). 1985. *Soviet Military Power*. Washington, D.C.: Government Printing Office.
European Security Study. 1983. *Strengthening Conventional Deterrence in Europe*. New York: St. Martin's Press.
Fallows, James. 1981. *National Defense*. New York: Random House.
Freedman, Lawrence. 1981. *The Evolution of Nuclear Strategy*. New York: St. Martin's Press.
Herken, Gregg. 1981. *The Winning Weapon: The Atomic Bomb in the Cold War, 1945–50*. New York: Random House/Vintage.
Hoffman, Stanley. 1979. "New Variations on Old Themes." *International Security*, vol. 4, no. 1 (Summer): 88–107.
———. 1983. *Dead Ends: American Foreign Policy in the New Cold War*, Chapter 11, "NATO and Nuclear Weapons." Cambridge, Mass.: Ballinger. Pp. 219–241.
IISS (International Institute for Strategic Studies). 1984. *The Military Balance 1984–85*. London: IISS.
Joffe, Josef. 1983. "Allies, Angst, and Arms Control: New Troubles for an Old Partnership." In *Nuclear Weapons in Europe*, Marsha McGraw Olive and Jeffrey D. Porro, eds. Lexington, Mass.: Lexington Books. Pp. 21–37.
Kaiser, Karl, Georg Leber, Alois Mertes, and Franz-Josef Schulze. 1982. "Nuclear Weapons and the Preservation of Peace." *Foreign Affairs*, vol. 60, no. 5 (Summer): 1157–1170.
Kaufmann, William W. 1983a. "Nuclear Deterrence in Central Europe." In *Alliance Security: NATO and the No-First-Use Question*, John D. Steinbruner and Leon V. Sigal, eds. Washington, D.C.: Brookings Institution. Pp. 22–42.
———. 1983b. "Nonnuclear Deterrence." In *Alliance Security: NATO and the No-First-Use Question*, John D. Steinbruner and Leon V. Sigal, eds. Washington, D.C.: Brookings Institution. Pp. 43–90.
Krell, Gert, Thomas Risse-Kappen, and Hans-Joachim Schmidt. 1983. "The No-First-Use Question in Germany." In *Alliance Security: NATO and the No-*

First-Use Question, John D. Steinbruner and Leon V. Sigal, eds. Washington, D.C.: Brookings Institution. Pp. 147–172.

Lambeth, Benjamin S. 1982/83. "Uncertainties for the Soviet War Planner." *International Security,* vol. 7, no. 3 (Winter): 139–166.

Lee, John Marshall. 1984. "The Use of Nuclear Weapons." Invited lecture at the Hubert Humphrey Institute of Public Affairs, University of Minnesota (November).

McNamara, Robert S. 1983. "The Military Role of Nuclear Weapons." *Foreign Affairs,* vol. 62, no. 1 (Fall): 59–80.

Mako, William P. 1983. *U.S. Ground Forces and the Defense of Central Europe.* Washington, D.C.: Brookings Institution.

Mearsheimer, John J. 1982. "Why the Soviets Can't Win Quickly in Central Europe." *International Security,* vol. 7, no. 1 (Summer): 3–39.

———. 1983. *Conventional Deterrence.* Ithaca, N.Y.: Cornell University Press.

———. 1984/85. "Nuclear Weapons and Deterrence in Europe." *International Security,* vol. 9, no. 3 (Winter): 19–46.

Nield, Robert. 1984. "European Security." In *The Arms Race at a Time of Decision: Annals of Pugwash 1983,* Joseph Rotblat and Alessandro Pascolini, eds. London: Macmillan. Pp. 157–163.

Olive, Marsha, and Jeffrey D. Porro, eds. 1983. *Nuclear Weapons in Europe.* Lexington, Mass.: Lexington Books.

Rogers, Bernard W. 1982. "The Atlantic Alliance." *Foreign Affairs,* vol. 60, no. 5 (Summer): 1145–1156.

Rosenberg, David Alan. 1983. "The Origins of Overkill: Nuclear Weapons and American Strategy 1945–60." *International Security,* vol. 7, no. 4 (Spring): 3–71.

Schmidt, Helmut. 1978. 'The 1977 Alastair Buchan Memorial Lecture." *Survival,* vol. 20 (January/February): 2–10.

Schwartz, David N. 1983. "A Historical Perspective." In *Alliance Security: NATO and the No-First-Use Question,* John D. Steinbruner and Leon V. Sigal, eds. Washington, D.C.: Brookings Institution. Pp. 5–21.

Sharp, Jane. 1984. "Mutual Force Reduction Negotiations." In *The Arms Race at a Time of Decision: Annals of Pugwash 1983,* Joseph Rotblat and Alessandro Pascolini, eds. London: Macmillan. Pp. 148–156.

Sigal, Leon V. 1983a. "No First Use and NATO's Nuclear Posture." In *Alliance Security: NATO and the No-First-Use Question,* John D. Steinbruner and Leon V. Sigal, eds. Washington, D.C.: Brookings Institution. Pp. 106–133.

———. 1983b. "Political Prospects for No First Use." In *Alliance Security: NATO and the No-First-Use Question,* John D. Steinbruner and Leon V. Sigal, eds. Washington, D.C.: Brookings Institution. Pp. 134–146.

Steinbruner, John D., and Leon V. Sigal, eds. 1983. *Alliance Security: NATO and the No-First-Use Question.* Washington, D.C.: Brookings Institution.

Union of Concerned Scientists (John Marshall Lee, Study Director). 1983. *No First Use.* Cambridge, Mass.: UCS.

York, Herbert F. 1983. "Beginning Nuclear Disarmament at the Bottom." *Survival,* vol. 25 (September/October): 227–231.

Zuckerman, Lord Solly. 1982. *Nuclear Illusion and Reality.* New York: Viking.

6

Star Wars and Arms Control

Sidney D. Drell

I am a scientist and I recognize the wisdom of Albert Einstein's remark that "politics is much harder than physics." Nevertheless, scientists do play an important role in analyzing the problems that the United States and its allies must consider regarding the Strategic Defense Initiative (SDI). For one thing we have valuable insights and understanding about the contribution of science to so technically advanced and ambitious a venture. But equally important, we can help clarify the limits of technology in our common effort to reduce the threat and the danger of nuclear weapons.

My assessment of the full magnitude of the technical challenge—and of the even more awesome operational challenge of developing a fully integrated operating system against a foe determined to defeat it with appropriate and available countermeasures—leads me to an important conclusion about strategic defense: There is no prospect of building an effective nationwide defense now or of achieving one in the foreseeable future unless the offensive threat is tightly constrained technically and greatly reduced numerically as a result of major progress in the political process and East-West arms control dialogue. The challenge of strategic defense is more than a technical and operational one. It is above all a political challenge to succeed in limiting offensive forces while simultaneously developing defenses to stop them.

My remarks about the opportunities and dangers in strategic defense—that is, what we should be doing and what we should not be doing—focus on the remainder of the twentieth century. Beyond then my vision is less certain; concerning the rest of this century, however, I base my discussion on four assumptions about the political, military, and technical situation.

1. There will be no fundamental or drastic change in the relationship between the United States and the Soviet Union; or between NATO

and the Warsaw Pact nations. We will remain adversaries and will continue to compete with one another at the same time as we strive to reduce the possibility of confrontation.
2. The strategic military balance will continue to be predicated on nuclear deterrence, which in turn is predicated on the dominance of offensive nuclear weapons. In consequence, entire societies will continue to be vulnerable.
3. The SALT I ABM treaty will continue to prove valuable for structuring U.S. and Soviet forces on a stable deterrent basis.
4. Large-scale research and development (R&D) projects might bring some individual strategic defense weapons systems or key components to the requisite performance capabilities by the turn of the century or later. However, the achievement of a fully effective and operational nationwide ballistic missile defense (BMD) system is highly conjectural at best because it depends on making technical advances that can only be characterized as revolutionary.

Technical and Operational Challenges

I am not a "naysayer" when it comes to technology. I enthusiastically supported the challenge of putting a man on the moon in the U.S. Apollo program, and I was confident of success. That program is often pointed to as an example of science and technology successfully meeting great challenges—but the analogy to strategic defense is badly flawed. Putting a man on the moon was solely a technical challenge. The moon couldn't shoot back, or run away, or dispense moon decoys, or turn off its lights. In other words it was not an active opponent determined to defeat the moonlander with countermeasures. In contrast, a strategic defense must work reliably in a hostile environment. We must establish and maintain high confidence in such an exceedingly complex system and its ability to accomplish its enormous task of battle management in a very short time even though it can never be tested under realistic conditions, such as in an environment disturbed by nuclear explosions.

Even if SDI meets its stated ambitious technical goals in a successful R&D program, severe operational problems will have to be mastered. Consider the challenge of boost-phase intercept, which is a crucial new ingredient of the envisaged strategic defense. This is the first of the three or four successive tiers or layers of the defense concept that is proposed, designed to destroy most of the attacking missiles over the enemy's own territory within seconds after they are launched—that is, during the boost phase while their engines are still accelerating them into space. Boost-phase intercept is considered an essential component of any defensive system able to respond effectively to an unconstrained threat as stated in the official Department of Defense report to the U.S. Congress in April 1985.

Suffice it to say that, as interesting or intriguing as the concept of boost-phase intercept may be, its realization lies well in the future, orders of magnitude beyond modern technology. Even if realized, boost-phase intercept would remain sensitive to countermeasures available to the offense. In particular, a boost-phase defense must start and complete its mission in seconds. At present only a few minutes at most are available to engage missiles during boost, but the technology to shorten the total burn time to less than one minute already exists. This means that the interceptors will have to be pre-deployed in space, or they will have to arrive very, very quickly. If they are in space, their numbers must necessarily be very large because only a small fraction of them will be on-station within range of Soviet launch areas at any one time. And they themselves will be more vulnerable than the missiles that are their targets because they move in predictable orbits.

These disadvantages of space basing have suggested that we look to the possibility of basing the interceptors on the ground, poised to "pop up" into space upon notification of enemy launch. The only practical device compact and light enough is the X-ray laser pumped by a nuclear explosive, but at present our physical understanding of the potential of such devices is much too primitive to draw any definite conclusions about its feasibility. Moreover, consider the necessary operational concept: Because the earth is round and one cannot peer over the horizon to see a rising booster, such a system would have to be based on submarines, close to the Soviet shoreline, able to respond instantaneously to the launch of an attacking missile.

We also should remember that the laws of physics are not secret; they cannot be classified. The possibilities of such lasers are well recognized by Soviet scientists. They have written about these concepts, as have U.S. scientists. The Soviets will build such devices if Americans do, probably not very long after, and surely long before the U.S. system is fully operational. It is ironic but not surprising that the widely heralded technology that first triggered so much interest in Star Wars is de-emphasized by the U.S. administration's stated goal of developing a nonnuclear defensive system. In fact, its most practical application could well be as an anti-satellite weapon (ASAT) against an opponent's Star Wars defenses.

This illustrates another technical problem of defense: It will rely necessarily on space-based sensors for its eyes and ears, even if the weapons themselves are not space-based. These sensors will then be vulnerable to ASATs. But as we develop strategic defenses, ASATs will be a ready by-product, unavoidably so because their task is simpler.

Therefore, developing SDI will lead to ASATs, which themselves threaten the space-based assets of SDI.

Other schemes for accomplishing boost-phase intercept have been proposed, but all have potentially vulnerable components—for example, large orbiting mirrors or particle accelerators based in space—or have very little, if any, time for accomplishing their intercept. Another of the severe technical difficulties is that of distinguishing warheads from decoys during mid-course flight above the atmosphere. There are several means, including nuclear weapons in various deployment modes and nonnuclear hit-to-kill projectiles (such as the one tested in the Homing Overlay Experiment), by which the defense might kill warheads, or reentry vehicles (RVs), in midcourse. Most of these means seem reasonable as potential components of military systems, provided their targets can be uniquely identified. However, no one has yet solved the original problem that plagued the Nike Zeus project in the late 1950s—how to tell the real RVs from decoys and sensor noise. There are currently numerous suggestions for solving the discrimination problem with both active and passive optics of various descriptions and with more exotic means such as high-energy particle beams and specially designed nuclear weapons, but no solution is in hand today. Moreover our ability to predict the effects of high-altitude nuclear explosions is currently insufficient to permit confident assessment of the performance of virtually any ABM system for accomplishing the difficult task of discrimination after the first few nuclear explosions at high altitudes.

For these basic reasons I see no prospect of building an effective nationwide defense now or of achieving one in the foreseeable future, unless the offensive threat is tightly constrained technically and greatly reduced numerically as a result of major progress in the U.S.-Soviet political process and dialogue.

On the basis of physics alone, one cannot say that strategic defense is impossible. There is no law of physics on which to base a claim that the cost exchange ratio between offense and defense will never favor defense. At present, however, such a favorable exchange ratio has not been established. Nor has it been established that we know how to build survivable defenses. The current and foreseeable technical situation therefore indicates that a movement toward a defense-dominant condition can be pursued with any hope of success only if restraints on offensive forces can be achieved through diplomacy, that is, through progress in arms control.

Deployment of Defensive Systems

The importance of this arms control framework is apparent as one looks ahead toward possible deployments of defensive systems. As Ambassador Paul Nitze remarked in a speech to the Philadelphia World Affairs Council on February 20, 1985, if the Star Wars research program of the administration is fully successful in developing new technologies that satisfy the two criteria of survivability and cost-effectiveness, then a decade or more from now we can look forward to entering a transition period during which defensive weapons will begin to be deployed in conjunction with offensive forces. This, he said, would be a "tricky" enterprise, and he added, "We would see the transition period as a cooperative endeavor with the Soviets. Arms control would play a critical role."

There is a policy issue in addition to the technical ones: No one has yet figured out how to make the transition from offense to defense dominance while retaining stability and avoiding a buildup of offensive weapons such as was triggered by the initial Soviet ABM deployments around Moscow in the 1960s that led to multiple, independently targeted reentry vehicles (MIRVs). Evidently, we will require an arms control regime in order to get anywhere with defensive deployments. Thus the strategic defense programs in the 1990s must not contribute to further eroding, or dismantling, our current treaty achievements. We should be working to strengthen the ABM Treaty because we will need it for the foreseeable future. We must at least reach an understanding with the Soviet Union as to what research in the new technologies is allowed and what activities are restrained by the ABM Treaty. This is currently an important issue because the United States government, while insisting that the SDI program will be fully compliant with the ABM Treaty, has raised questions about the treaty interpretation and whether its provisions restrain the development and testing of the new technologies, such as lasers and directed energy weapons.

The 1985 report of the Defense Department to Congress on the SDI program has already raised this issue by proposing experiments that exploit some of the inevitable verbal ambiguities in the 1972 treaty. For example, Article V of the treaty forbids development, testing, or deployment of "ABM systems or components" that are space-based or air-based. At issue is how far one can go in disaggregating components into subcomponents in order to claim compliance. Is it allowable to test an airborne or space-based sensor against a warhead so long as it lacks a direct communication link to the ground? Is it legal for an airborne or space-based missile interceptor to be tested against a satellite, just not against an intercontinental ballistic missile (ICBM) warhead? Or may it be tested against a warhead, so long as it doesn't carry its own target-tracking system? How can one develop space-based high velocity interceptors (kinetic kill vehicles or railguns) consistent with Article V?

What about the Soviets? They have an ongoing program in ABM technology and, in accord with the ABM Treaty, have deployed and are upgrading a limited system around Moscow. They are also constructing a large radar at Krasnoyarsk that is similar to their other early warning radars—but because it is not being located at the periphery looking outward from the Soviet Union it appears to be a violation of treaty provisions. They are also engaged in research on directed energy weapons. And, although the Soviet program in directed energy research may be judged comparable to that of the United States, the Soviets lag in other technologies that are crucial for ABM systems. According to the U.S. Department of Defense,[1] the United States has a lead in computers, optics, automated control, electro-optical sensors, propulsion, radar, software, telecommunications, and guidance systems. The only area in which the Soviet Union is said to enjoy a substantial lead is in large rockets that could lift heavy loads into space. The level of Soviet technology suggests that if the Soviet Union tried to break out of the ABM Treaty by deploying an advanced ABM system, it could not develop an effective system so rapidly as to deprive the United States of its ability to deliver a massive retaliatory strike. I disagree with claims that the U.S. program in SDI is necessary in order to catch up with the Soviets.

SDI and the NATO Alliance

The U.S. policy and program with regard to SDI raises three specific and important issues for our alliance partners. The first is technology transfer. The ABM Treaty prohibits the "transfer to other states" of "ABM systems or their components" or of "technical descriptions or blueprints" worked out for their construction. These provisions prohibit the signatory nations from using their allies to circumvent ABM Treaty constraints. As a result, allied participation in a treaty-compliant research program would have to be limited to research that had not reached the "system" or "component" level. More of a problem for research at this stage would be restrictions that the United States itself might impose, as it does now, in the transfer of military technology to its allies for fear that such technologies may eventually reach the Soviet Union.

The second issue has to do with implications for the independent nuclear deterrents of the United Kingdom and France. These forces present a threat to the Soviet Union of much smaller magnitude than the full strategic forces of the superpowers. Will a transition to a defensive strategy result in a diminution in their importance and effectiveness?

The third issue is the defense of our allies. In Europe specifically, will the technology of SDI lead to the development of effective defenses against shorter-range tactical ballistic missiles? The technical problems of defense against such a threat differ from those for a defense against long-range strategic missiles because tactical missiles fly on very different trajectories. How practical is it to achieve a defense of societies or of the battlefield against the threat of medium-range nuclear-tipped missiles?

Conclusion

I support a deliberately paced U.S. defense effort on strategic defense, organized and pursued with clearly stated goals and means, abiding by the ABM Treaty. Such a program should serve our security at reasonable cost. The current budget of $2.75 billion for fiscal year 1986, which represents a doubling of the program expenditures from 1985, is more than adequate for a robust, efficient, and high-quality research program. Such a U.S. program should give the Soviet government—itself engaged in R&D on strategic defenses—no reason to feel the need for additional offensive or defensive forces in response. A U.S. effort with better planning, explanation, and diplomacy might moderate Soviet concerns and their perceptions, which now regard the U.S. program as threatening their deterrent capability, menacing strategic stability, and defeating the prospects for arms control. It would also be of enormous value for the Soviets to take some reciprocal steps to explain some of their troubling actions, including in particular discussion of the Krasnoyarsk radar. More openness in this dialogue would be immensely valuable.

The impact of such clearly defined and constrained activities on the ABM Treaty should be nil, in the near- and mid-terms. Genuine success in creating a new approach to effective nationwide strategic defense would indeed present a challenge to the ABM Treaty. If this should occur, it would do so well into the future, regardless of which side succeeded in developing the defensive system. The United States and its allies would need to conceive and negotiate a new arms control regime that would successfully integrate offensive and defensive forces.

Above all, I urge that society once again step back and view the threat of nuclear weapons in proper perspective. The difficulty is much deeper and the solution much more radical than can be solved by technology; diplomacy must play a part in progress toward a safer world. History reminds us of how grave the danger is, for over the full span of human records there have been wars, and in them we have used every means available at the time to overpower and kill one another. We are witness to tragic and brutal conflicts at this very time. Our challenge is thus not to make a better laser or computer. For the United States and the Soviet Union, especially, as possessors of close to 99 percent of the world's nuclear weapons, the challenge is to be serious—really serious—and committed to improving our political, diplomatic, and human relations. We must face our common danger—nuclear weapons. Avoiding a nuclear holocaust is a deep moral obligation we bear to generations yet unborn.

Notes

1. See (1) The FY1986 Department of Defense Program for Research, Development, and Acquisition. Statement by the Under Secretary of Defense for Research and Engineering, Ninety-ninth Congress, first session, 1985, p. II-4, and (2) United States Military Posture FY1986. Annual Report. The Organization of the Joint Chiefs of Staff.

7

Which SDI?

Eckhard Lübkemeier

In assessing the Strategic Defense Initiative (SDI), it is useful to distinguish between two levels: (1) a total defense—President Reagan's March 23, 1983, vision of an impermeable defense system that would render nuclear weapons "impotent and obsolete," and (2) a limited defense—a ballistic missile defense (BMD) system that would provide little or no protection for the population but would be capable of defending certain military facilities against ballistic missile attack.

Public debate about SDI continues to focus primarily on the first level, for essentially two reasons. First, the popular appeal of SDI hinges largely on the hope that SDI will, in the long run, free the world from the curse of nuclear weapons. This hope is a natural and understandable response to the prospect that we may be forced to live for another forty or more years in the shadow of nuclear annihilation. Second, the Reagan administration continues to support the idea of an impermeable defense system. In his speech to the United Nations on October 24, 1985, for example, President Reagan said that "the world will sleep more secure when these missiles will have been rendered useless, politically and militarily ineffective, when the sword of Damocles that has been hanging over our planet all too long will have been removed by Western and Russian scientists."[1] Although noble, President Reagan's vision is unreachable through the SDI program. I cannot offer a complete discussion of this topic here because of space limitations and the need to cover the military-strategic and arms control aspects of SDI. A brief discussion will suffice.

A close reading of official SDI publications and statements by representatives of the administration gives one the distinct impression that many officials support the goal of a nuclear-free world more as a statement of loyalty to President Reagan than of genuine conviction that nuclear weapons can be rendered obsolete. The emphasis is not on overcoming deterrence based on the capability of nuclear retaliation but on "how deterrence can be enhanced through a greater reliance on new defensive systems."[2] The 1985 Pentagon report on SDI speaks of eliminating "the threat posed by ballistic missiles" as one of the goals of SDI, but then goes on to state without further qualification that "SDI seeks, therefore, to exploit emerging technologies that may provide options for a *broader-based* deterrence by turning to a *greater* reliance on defensive systems"[3] (emphasis added).

This less ambitious objective recognizes that the effective protection of the U.S. population would require a nearly leakproof defense against a Soviet nuclear attack. The Office of Technology Assessment (OTA) has determined that, if the Soviets intended to kill Americans, a mere one percent of Soviet nuclear weapons would suffice to inflict casualties well in excess of 10 million.[4] The OTA calculations are, of course, based on assumptions that are subject to change (for example, the number of Soviet offensive nuclear arms). Nevertheless, it is difficult to disagree with the view that, given the enormous destructive potential of just one nuclear weapon, a nuclear warhead that successfully permeated a defensive shield would most certainly be one warhead too many.

However, even Reagan administration officials have expressed serious doubts about the technological feasibility of an impermeable defense system. The director of the SDI Organization, Lieutenant General James Abrahamson, for instance, freely admits that some warheads would get through.[5] In all probability, and contrary to Secretary of Defense Caspar Weinberger's hope, SDI "will not free the world from the dark shadow that has been cast over it since the emergence of nuclear weapons."[6] At least for the foreseeable future, the SDI program seems above all to be geared to exploring and developing BMD technologies that will add a defensive component to a deterrent strategy that heretofore has been almost exclusively based on offensive weapons. It would be misleading, however, to dismiss President Reagan's vision as an illusion that is technically unfeasible and hence of no political relevance. To the contrary, in this chapter I will demonstrate that it is indeed this vision of nuclear liberation that gives the SDI program its politically and militarily explosive character.

The following analysis of the military-strategic and arms control policy implications of SDI will focus on three areas: strategic deterrence, extended deterence, and arms control. In each case, pro-SDI arguments will be introduced and analyzed. The discussion is based on the assumption that a leakproof BMD system is unattainable and therefore that, for purposes of deterrence, we will have to continue to rely on the threat of nuclear retaliation.

Strategic Deterrence

THESIS: The stability of deterrence by offensive nuclear weapons is prone to erosion in the long run.

Essentially, there are two rationales for this argument. The first is the assertion, derived from Soviet armament policy, that the Soviet Union has never accepted the principle of deterrence by mutual assured destruction (MAD). Moscow is said to cling to the view that even in the nuclear age effective deterrence requires a capability to fight and win a nuclear war. In particular, the Soviet buildup of accurate ICBMs is seen as evidence of this attitude, allegedly threatening the survivability of U.S. ICBMs and large portions of the U.S. command, control, and communications structure. To the U.S. administration, this "pattern of activity suggest[s] that the continued long-term dependence on offensive forces may not provide a stable basis for deterrence."[7]

The second rationale, propagated above all by Under Secretary of Defense for Policy Fred Iklé, is more fundamental. "Relying on an imagined consensus with a partner not to defend oneself while renewing incessantly one's capabilities to destroy that partner, is not a plausible, and not a desirable basis for a stable strategic relationship. It is far more likely that we and the Soviets could agree to reduce offensive forces while allowing each other to have effective defenses. Such a relationship would meet the priority objective of any rational government—to protect its homeland."[8]

The argument that the Soviet armament policy precludes a lasting and stable system of deterrence rests on several dubious assumptions. Among them is the assertion advanced recently by the head of the planning office of the West German Department of Defense, Hans Rühle, that the Soviet Union could use its ICBMs to destroy 2,000 targets in the United States (among them probably all of the approximately 1,000 ICBMs) with a 95 percent probability of success.[9] Such calculations are based on many factors that are difficult to quantify. The uncertainties relate, for instance, to the so-called fratricide effect, that is, the possibility that detonating warheads may destroy other incoming warheads, and to the fact that a massive employment of nuclear arms can never be tested beforehand—missiles have to be launched on untried trajectories. Adding to this uncertainty, any Soviet decisionmaker must contemplate the possibility that the United States may launch on warning, a policy Washington has not ruled out.

Much more serious than these technical problems, however, is the question of the strategic significance of a putative Soviet capability to completely or almost completely wipe out land-based U.S. nuclear forces in a first strike. Would such an option give the Soviet Union an advantage that could be exploited politically or militarily? It cannot be denied, especially in view of the accuracy of modern ballistic missiles, that the vulnerability of the immobile components of U.S. and Soviet nuclear arsenals (silo-hardened ICBMs; command, control, and communications facilities; bombers at air bases; and submarines in ports) has grown. Currently owing to its numerous accurate ICBM warheads, the Soviet Union probably has a greater capability than the United States to destroy fixed and hardened military targets.[10] President Reagan used this U.S. "window of vulnerability" in his 1980 election campaign to blame the Carter administration for neglecting U.S. security interests.

According to the underlying scenario, the Soviet ICBMs would destroy U.S. ICBMs and thus the only means available to the United States for selective retaliatory strikes. Because the U.S. casualties would not be high enough to cause massive U.S. retaliation and because the U.S. president's only remaining nuclear assets would not be suitable for a damage-limiting retaliation, the president would be faced with the decision of having to surrender or escalate to all-out nuclear war. The scenario does not necessarily imply that the Soviet Union really intends to launch such an attack. It is feared, however, that in a crisis a U.S. president might succumb to Soviet coercion as the result of U.S. counterforce inferiority.

The main flaw in this argument is the assumption that the Soviet leadership would expect a U.S. president to accept without retaliation a Soviet counterforce attack resulting in "only" a few million deaths. Even administration officials admit implicitly that it would hardly be possible to present plausible evidence for this. General Abrahamson, for example, included the Soviet Union in his observation that "military people are quite conservative when it comes to your country and your way of life. No one is going to likely enter into one of these kinds of terrible nuclear exchanges."[11] Similarly, President Reagan's Science Adviser George Keyworth II maintained that "no military planner would seriously contemplate a first strike unless he had very high confidence that his opponent would be crippled by it—that is, unable to retaliate."[12]

The "window of vulnerability" is therefore the kind of nuclear war scenario that is more likely to strengthen than undermine one's confidence in the stability of deterrence.[13] As long as both sides have an assured retaliatory capability, limited nuclear attacks will not lead to any decisive military advantage, whereas partially disarming strikes (for instance, against an opponent's immobile strategic assets) or incapacitating attacks against command and communications facilities run the risk of a devastating retaliation.

Moreover, it is interesting to note that the Reagan administration's actual arms policy confirms that the ICBM vulnerability problem is not taken as seriously as the above-mentioned scenario suggests. Indeed, the Reagan administration plans to station the new MX missiles in existing silos and now pursues a ban on mobile ICBMs at the bargaining table in Geneva. What is more, SDI itself does little to alleviate the vulnerability problem in the near term because, according to the administration, the "primary thrust of the SDI research program is not to focus on generating options for the earliest development/deployment decision. . . . The goal of our research is not, and cannot be, simply to protect our retaliatory forces from attack."[14]

This objective reveals again the dubious nature of the allegation that "the aggregate of the USSR's ABM and ABM-related activities suggests that the USSR may be preparing an ABM defense of its national territory."[15] If there were a real danger of the Soviet Union gaining a strategic advantage through a breakout from the ABM Treaty, the administration would hardly focus its SDI activities on research for technologies that can bear military fruit only in the long term. It is no wonder, then, that Paul Nitze believes [the Soviets] "could have something by 1990 that would be a partial defense of their national territory, though it would not be something which we could not overwhelm."[16] There is apparently no need for grave concern in another field that is significant for the survivabililty of the U.S. nuclear deterrent. Analysts for the National Intelligence Council "do not believe there is a realistic possibility that the Soviets will be able to deploy in the 1990s a system that could pose any significant threat to U.S. SSBNs [ballistic missile nuclear submarines] on patrol."[17]

A realistic analysis of the impact of past and prospective Soviet offensive and defensive programs leads to the conclusion that U.S. deterrent forces, when taken as a whole, are not in jeopardy. Because the same holds for the Soviet Union, the deterrence founded on the mutually assured capability of retaliation will continue to enjoy a high degree of stability. Hence, pro-SDI arguments based on the opposite view rest on shaky ground.

This can also be said of the argument advanced by Iklé. He points out that the dichotomy between enemy and partner inherent in nuclear deterrence is a potential source of instability. Although this diagnosis is essentially correct, Iklé's prescription of developing a defense-based deterrent is misleading. Even that type of system would not be suited to protect against the antagonistic conflict of values and interests between East and West. Because there is no prospect of rendering nuclear weapons "impotent and obsolete" by technical means, the only way out is through a political strategy directed towards détente. Deterrence policy is part of such a strategy but it cannot substitute for a political solution to international conflicts.

THESIS: The deployment of BMD systems will put deterrence on a more stable basis.

In my opinion, the current system of deterrence is and continues to be more effective than the Reagan administration pretends it to be. This assessment does not necessarily speak against the utility of BMD systems. For one, the speedy development and deployment of counterforce weapons on either side raises legitimate concern among experts and the public alike, especially with regard to crisis stability. Second, the risk of war will remain high even if the likelihood of its breaking out is very low: If deterrence does fail, humanity's survival is at stake. Thus any military measure that could contribute to reducing the probability of war should in principle be welcome. The proponents of SDI maintain that the deployment of defensive systems will reduce the probability of war. According to this line of argument, defensive systems enhance deterrence insofar as they "exacerbate the uncertainty of a potential attacker in his ability to succeed in his attack by presenting him with a complex defense suppression problem."[18]

However, in certain circumstances BMD systems may even result in a loss of stability, a problem alluded to by President Reagan himself on March 23, 1983: "If paired with offensive systems, [defensive systems] can be viewed as fostering an aggressive policy, and no one wants that."[19] The potentially perilous element of a combination of offensive counterforce weapons with BMD installations could be that in a crisis either side may have an additional incentive for preemptive action.

> A point might be reached where one or both sides could achieve a damage limitation capability, but would possess it only if they struck first. Such a first strike would overcome the adversary's defenses and destroy the vulnerable portions of the adversary's offensive forces.
>
> If the adversary attempted to strike back with the remaining portion of its strategic offensive forces, it would not be able to overcome the attacker's defenses.[20]

Administration officials such as President Reagan's former National Security Adviser Robert McFarlane and Special Adviser on Arms Control Paul Nitze have repeatedly referred to such a danger,[21] thus confirming that defensive systems are not inherently "good" weapons simply because they would threaten only other weapons instead of people. Defensive weapons could instead enhance the efficacy of offensive weapons in a first-strike mode, especially if essential elements of the BMD system were vulnerable to attack.²² Mainly for this reason administration figures such as Nitze advocate a cooperative defensive transition. There is little likelihood, however, that the Soviet Union will be persuaded to deploy defensive systems parallel to cuts in offensive arms.

President Reagan stated that he reassured General Secretary Gorbachev during their Geneva summit "that if our research reveals that a defense against nuclear missiles is possible, we would sit down with our allies and the Soviet Union to see how together we could replace all strategic ballistic missiles with such a defense, which threatens no one."²³ The Soviet leadership, however, is unlikely to ignore the strings attached to this by Pentagon officials. Secretary Weinberger, for instance, interpreted the above-mentioned presidential statement as follows:

> I don't think that the President has ever said or indicated that any vital technology that is not already known to the Soviet Union would be handed over.
>
> The whole idea that he has in mind is that if you both have thoroughly reliable defensive systems—and bear in mind that the Soviets have been working on it about sixteen years now very intensively—it is desirable that there be a form of planned deployment, a 'negotiated deployment' in the sense that ways in which the defensive installations would be handled could bring greater stability.²⁴

And Richard Perle, an assistant secretary of defense, went so far as to suggest that an agreement about sharing SDI technology would only be possible if "no significant threat [existed] to the United States." A "massive disarmament" of offensive weapons would have to occur first.²⁵

Statements such as these will no doubt strengthen the position of those in the USSR who believe that cooperation with the United States is not possible or that it can only occur on acceptable terms if the Soviet Union will not assume a *demandeur* position. To avoid getting into such a situation and to preserve their deterrent, the Soviets are likely to upgrade their strategic forces in the area in which they excel already—the realm of offensive ballistic missiles. Thus, instead of inducing the Soviets to shift their forces to a more defensive posture, SDI may drive Moscow to build ever more and more offensive weapons.

The possible impact on deterrence stability of such a Soviet response is hard to assess. Although SDI is geared to research in technologies with long-term implications, the United States in the meantime still plans to modernize its offensive forces and maintain an adequate deterrent. But the development of strong U.S. offensive forces, along with a superior BMD capability, could then be interpreted by the Soviets as fostering the kind of aggressive policy that, in President Reagan's words, "no one wants."

The potential stability problems associated with a progressive deployment of defensive systems can therefore be avoided only if these systems are deployed by the United States and the Soviet Union in a coordinated fashion. Here, the U.S. government is faced with a dilemma that goes back to the goal of "rendering nuclear weapons impotent and obsolete." As long as the United States challenges the future viability of the current deterrence system, and as long as Soviet arms and arms control policy is conducted within the framework of this system, cooperation cannot be expected. On the other hand, the development and deployment of BMD systems in confrontation with the USSR could seriously compromise strategic stability and U.S. security. But if the administration abandons its ultimate goal of a world free of nuclear arms, SDI would lose a great deal of its popular appeal; arms control agreements or even unilateral nondefensive action (for instance, the development of mobile ICBMs) could enhance the stability of a deterrence regime dominated by offensive weapons.

THESIS: A BMD system would reduce damage if deterrence should fail.

Deterrence could fail because of nuclear war between the United States and the USSR, attack by a third nation, or accidental or unauthorized attack.[26]

The prospects of limiting civilian casualties by a less-than-total missile defense are slim if the Soviet Union targets its arms massively on U.S. cities. If deterrence were to fail, such strikes might become even more likely if attacks on military targets could be intercepted by a limited BMD system.

In order to reliably intercept deliberate or accidental limited attacks by the other superpower or by third nations, a defense system would have to come close to comprehensive ballistic defense. A system exclusively capable of protecting military targets would not do because even limited counter-city strikes would result in intolerably high casualties. For this reason, such a system would probably require at least one space-based component. It appears unlikely, however, that such a component could be so designed and deployed that the other side would not perceive it as diminishing its second-strike capability and thus its deterrent.

In spite of all this, there remains, of course, the chance that some form of BMD system may indeed be able to limit damage from a limited missile attack. But in the strategic realm, such scenarios remain highly unlikely because limited attacks by one superpower against the other would be coupled with an extraordinarily high risk of escalation. Moreover, Third World nations are unlikely to compete against the superpowers in the nuclear realm; instead, they would acquire nuclear weapons for regional threats and contingencies. In this case, I therefore fully share the all-or-nothing philosophy of SDI: In nuclear war a BMD system will be useless unless it insures flawless protection for the population; anything less, that is, a limited defense, is not worth the effort.

Extended Deterrence

The United States has committed itself to safeguarding Western Europe's security, even with nuclear weapons. With regard to the implications of SDI for extended deterrence it is necessary to take into account first the two levels of SDI defined at the beginning of this chapter.

At the first level, two different cases are conceivable. If the United States were able to achieve invulnerability from nuclear attack while the Soviet Union remained exposed to U.S. nuclear arms, the United States would have restored its former nuclear superiority. This, according to proponents of SDI, would strengthen extended deterrence because, in the case of a Soviet attack against Western Europe, Moscow would have to reckon with an increased U.S. readiness to employ nuclear weapons from behind its impermeable shield. If, on the other hand, the Soviet Union could also find sanctuary behind a leakproof defense system, security for both Western Europe and the non-Soviet nations of Eastern Europe would diminish. The development of a defense that would protect the densely populated European nations with their sensitive infrastructure against a host of Soviet nuclear weapons seems even more impossible. But even if Europe could be shielded from nuclear attack, the possibility of a conventional war that both superpowers could wage without risk of nuclear escalation would still remain. In view of NATO's often underrated conventional strength, the probability of such a war or a tactical-nuclear conflict between the United States and the Soviet Union conducted in the European theater would still have to be considered low; nevertheless, such a war could become more likely if the leading powers of the two blocs would no longer sit in the same boat with their European allies.

I believe that neither the United States nor the USSR will succeed in achieving immunity from nuclear attack. The relevance of SDI for extended deterrence and NATO's strategy of flexible response, therefore, has to be analyzed in the context of a limited BMD system with limited effectiveness. What impact could such a system have on the security of nonnuclear West European states such as the Federal Republic of Germany?

THESIS: The credibility of extended deterrence increases if U.S. vulnerability to nuclear attack decreases.

This argument centers on the sore point of the U.S. nuclear guarantee for Western Europe:[27] Is the United States willing to risk its own existence for a third country? Obviously, West Europeans are interested in giving the U.S. nuclear guarantee maximum credibility in the eyes of the Soviet leadership. The question, then, is whether a limited strategic BMD capability could enhance the deterrent effect of this guarantee.

If the United States alone had a defense capability against limited nuclear attack, it could implement what in NATO parlance is called a "politically controlled, selective use of nuclear weapons" without having to fear a Soviet response in kind. Such an advantage for the United States, however, would have a serious drawback for Western Europe. The Soviet Union could well threaten to respond to a limited U.S. nuclear strike by massive retaliation against Western Europe, thus placing Western Europe in a situation similar to its position in the 1950s when the United States was superior in long-range nuclear weapons.

In all likelihood, the Soviet Union will want to avoid a strategic situation in which it would have to rely on holding third countries hostage to ensure parity with the United States. Therefore, it can be expected to follow suit and deploy its own limited ballistic missile defense. This need not lead to a complete decoupling of Western Europe from the United States because nuclear war could still escalate and spill over into Soviet territory. However, the effectiveness of extended deterrence could be impaired if the Soviets were able to deploy a defense against ballistic missiles, cruise missiles, and aircraft that would make the selective use of nuclear weapons more difficult. Because NATO could no longer be certain which of its nuclear weapons would reach their targets, any employment of nuclear weapons aimed at controlling escalation and avoiding collateral damage would involve greater risks than at present. In the Soviet view, this could diminish U.S. readiness to employ nuclear weapons for the defense of Western Europe, thus weakening extended deterrence.

Any discussion of the rather vague notion of deterrence credibility is by nature marked by speculation. Credibility is decided by the opponent on the basis of a contingent risk analysis. Hence, I do not assert that deployment of BMD systems by the United States and USSR would inevitably degrade the credibility of extended deterrence to a degree that would jeopardize Western Europe's security. But the inverse thesis need not be true either: Reduced U.S. vulnerability to Soviet nuclear strikes would not per se imply a strengthening of extended deterrence.

As in the INF modernization issue, this point demonstrates again that preserving the credibility of U.S. nuclear commitment is primarily a political, not a military, problem. U.S. readiness to make use of a military option that might lead to its own destruction will depend on Western Europe's political and strategic importance to the United States. There is no reason for the Soviet Union to assume that the United States would tolerate a Soviet attempt to forcibly change the status quo in Europe. Likewise, there is little evidence that the Soviet Union intends to run the risk of a military confrontation with the United States. The U.S. nuclear commitment to Western Europe will therefore continue to be adequately effective for the foreseeable future even without backup from a strategic BMD system.

THESIS: NATO's deterrence will be enhanced if the West improves its defense against Soviet arms.

The United States has pledged that "the SDI program will not confine itself solely to an exploitation of technologies with potential against ICBMs and SLBMs [submarine-launched ballistic missiles], but will also carefully examine technologies with potential against shorter range ballistic missiles."[28] Effective defense against such weapons would strengthen the West's ability to deter conventional as well as nuclear aggression because it "could reduce the ability of Soviet ballistic missiles to place at risk those facilities essential to a conventional defense of Europe, facilities such as airfields, ports, depots, and communications facilities."[29] This issue, too, can be adequately discussed only if the goal is clearly defined: Is there to be a European complement to the SDI vision or is it "only" a question of making NATO forces in Europe more resistant to the effects of enemy weapons? In the former case, the primary objective would be to protect the population; in the latter, to protect weapons.

For reasons mentioned above, it appears impossible to deploy a defense system that could keep casualties among the European civilian populations at "tolerable" levels. Such a system will at most give rise to a false sense of security. Even worse, it could decrease security, for both political and military reasons. Politically, a European Defense Initiative (EDI) complementing SDI could be perceived by the Soviets as an additional threat to their deterrent. In this case the USSR would hold the European allies of the United States accountable if the two superpowers were unable to agree on offensive and defensive arms control. EDI might also have adverse military consequences for NATO's conventional defense. The U.S. Supreme Allied Commander, Europe, General Bernard Rogers, and General Wolfgang Altenburg, the West German chief of staff, have voiced concern that the cost of strategic BMD systems may negatively affect the level of U.S. outlays for conventional forces in Europe.[30] And if West European governments decided to build an effective shield for their population, financial constraints would force them to cut back on conventional defense spending.

Protecting military installations against enemy firepower is a limited and generally legitimate objective. Any decision on what kind of and how much defense is useful in this respect should take into account the following criteria: feasibility, funding, cost-effectiveness, and the expected Warsaw Pact response. It is difficult to determine whether the results of a cost-benefit analysis based on these criteria would lead NATO to develop and deploy sophisticated defense systems. Aside from other reasons, financial constraints alone would seem to encourage European NATO countries to forgo development of such systems.

Arms Control

The U.S. government has announced that it is seeking an arms control regime with the Soviet Union that will provide for a stable transition to a defense-dominant strategic posture. SDI research is said to promote the chances of accomplishing such an understanding.

THESIS: The SDI program provides an incentive for strategic arms reduction and a transition to defensive systems.

The Reagan administration has made drastic cuts in strategic offensive weapons one of the major goals of its arms control policy. Above all, the policy seeks the reduction of the number of Soviet ICBMs, which are considered particularly destabilizing because of their presumed capability to destroy most U.S. ICBMs. SDI is believed to offer an incentive for the Soviets to cut their ICBM inventory if the feasibility of effective ballistic missile defense can be demonstrated.[31] Furthermore, proponents of SDI assert that the forced obsolescence of ballistic missiles would be useful even if it were to cause the Soviet Union to focus on other offensive weapons like aircraft and cruise missiles because these systems would bolster strategic stability.[32]

Significant cuts in strategic arms cannot be expected for the duration of the SDI research phase. The Soviet Union has declared its intention to upgrade and optimize its offensive arsenal if the United States goes ahead with SDI.[33] Although it will continue and perhaps intensify its own BMD research and development program,[34] the Soviet Union will presumably respond to SDI by focusing on offensive systems, perhaps combined with a BMD system based on traditional technologies. Several factors explain this probable Soviet response. First, the USSR already has the technical and industrial capacity to rapidly produce offensive weapons. Second, Soviet leaders surely recognize that they would be hard pressed to compete with the United States in the realm of advanced BMD technology. Finally, the Soviets no doubt hope that they can demonstrate to the United States the futility of a costly U.S. strategic defense effort with relatively inexpensive offensive weapons. This last reason must certainly work against any major shift in emphasis among the Soviet Union's offensive assets. If Moscow hopes to dissuade the United States from SDI, it will be important for the Soviet Union to demonstrate that a BMD system can be penetrated not only indirectly by aircraft and cruise missiles but also directly by ballistic missiles.

For these reasons it is more likely that we will witness an increase in instead of a reduction or restructuring of Soviet nuclear forces. At least for the rest of the 1980s, while heated debate and uncertainty about the technical feasibility of the SDI program continues in the West, one should not expect the Soviet Union to improve the political chances of the program through drastic cuts in its own offensive arsenal.

The U.S. government concedes that there is a substantial risk of an offensive arms buildup by the Soviets to counter SDI. To forestall such a reaction, a defense system must be efficient as well as cost-effective, that is, it "must be able to maintain a sufficient degree of effectiveness to fulfill its mission, even in the face of determined attacks against it. This characteristic is essential not only to maintain the effectiveness of a defense system, but to maintain stability."[35] How effectiveness is defined or can be defined, however, is not clear.

In view of geographical differences, divergent nuclear force structures, and different economic and political conditions, a program may be cost-effective for the Soviet Union that would not be so for the United States. In theory, the United States could try to strengthen its antimissile defense to such a degree that the deployment of additional offensive weapons by the USSR would be to no avail. Inversely, the Soviet Union could try to counter a U.S. BMD system by improving its offensive potential. The Reagan administration admits that it is not clear who would win in such an offensive-defensive race: "Judgments of technological feasibility and of possible costs (including offense/defense cost ratios) are highly premature."[36]

At any rate the Soviet Union will probably not give in early or easily but rather will go to great lengths to undercut the effectiveness of a U.S. BMD system. This, in turn, could drive the United States to modernize its offensive inventory as well in order to reinforce its second-strike capability and provide a military backup for the development and deployment of BMD installations carried out without Soviet cooperation.[37] Resources spent on offensive assets, however, would compete with funds for developing BMD components, a process that would surely intensify the debate surrounding the cost-effectiveness of BMD systems.

The cost-effectiveness criterion is closely related to the level of support the SDI enjoys in U.S. politics. Reliable estimates of the possible cost of a BMD system centered on space-based components cannot be made at present, but the funds necessary will certainly be substantial. During the first two budget years of the SDI program, Congress voted cuts of about 25 percent (of the approximately U.S. $1.8 billion requested for FY1985, $1.4 billion was appropriated, and the $3.7 billion requested for FY1986 was cut to $2.75 billion), and this may have been but a foretaste of the congressional resistance to the extraordinary sums necessary to move the program from the research to the development and deployment stage. The debate will be heavily influenced by the popularity of SDI among U.S. voters. According to a recent poll, 59 percent of Americans favor SDI, but 74 percent also thought it to be "a very important goal" to reach an arms control agreement "in which the U.S. stops building Star Wars defense systems and the Soviet Union makes similar cutbacks in its military systems."[38] Poll results such as these indicate that the Reagan administration has not yet succeeded in convincing the U.S. population to accept the SDI vision of nuclear invulnerability. Instead, the majority of Americans seem prepared to sacrifice this vision for an arms control agreement leading to more stability through fewer weapons within the existing system of offensive deterrence.

THESIS: SDI contributes to the prevention of Soviet violation and erosion of arms control agreements.

The U.S. government has repeatedly accused the USSR of violating arms control obligations. In particular, a major radar installation near Krasnoyarsk in Siberia is said to be incompatible with the provision of the ABM Treaty that restricts the deployment of early warning radars to the periphery of either national territory. In the view of the administration, the Krasnoyarsk radar and other Soviet BMD and BMD-related activities (upgrading and expansion of the BMD system around Moscow, extensive research into advanced BMD technologies, and modernization of strategic air defense) offer grounds for concern that the Soviets might be preparing a nationwide ballistic missile defense banned by the ABM Treaty. SDI is considered to be a necessary and powerful deterrent against such a violation.[39] Although space does not permit a thorough analysis of Soviet treaty compliance, it is important to note that the Krasnoyarsk radar is good evidence of the Soviet inclination to interpret and apply treaties according to the tenet "What is not expressively banned is permitted."[40] SDI, however, is unlikely to induce the Soviets to change this policy.

The SDI research phase itself involves grey-area activities that are difficult to reconcile with the ABM Treaty. In particular, the administration's policy of a limited interpretation of the term "ABM component," in order to gain more freedom for experiments, must be a cause of concern.[41] The credibility of the Reagan administration's commitment to the ABM Treaty is further jeopardized by a recent interpretation that allows the development and testing of ABM systems based on new physical principles. The administration has given assurances of continued adherence to the previous restrictive interpretation that only *research* in such technologies is permitted, but the ABM Treaty's fundamental approach ("what is not expressly permitted is banned") has suffered substantially from this legal turn of events.

The essential objection against the thesis that SDI would enhance Soviet treaty compliance, however, is implicit in the visionary goal of SDI. The United States and the USSR entered into the strategic arms control talks of the 1970s with the mutually shared conviction of the dominance of offense over defense. If the U.S. government now maintains that it no longer considers this relation to be inevitable, the basis for the ABM Treaty and the entire arms control process to date is called into question. This would hardly encourage the Soviet Union to comply with its legal and political commitment to the results of that process.

This argument should not be construed as a plea for ignoring or casually tolerating suspicious Soviet treaty practices. The Soviets must become more sensitive to the fact that adequate public support in the United States for arms control requires them to honor their treaty obligations in a manner that must be determined by a less legalistic and more political approach. But the military, political, and technological challenge posed by SDI to their superpower status is unlikely to promote such an adjustment.

Conclusion

The Strategic Defense Initiative may become a case of the best being the enemy of good. The best, of course, would be the total elimination of nuclear weapons, which will only be possible in a world where conflicts between nations no longer provoke arms competition. President Reagan's vision is based on the erroneous belief that such a change of the international system can be wrought by technological innovation. Even if one succeeded, against all odds, in finding a technological panacea guaranteeing complete protection against nuclear weapons, it would only safeguard the peace if it were developed and deployed in cooperation with the Soviet Union. Otherwise, this deus ex machina would be perceived by the USSR as a threat to its existence, which it would feel obliged to counter with all military or political means available. In this way, the bird in the hand—an agreed stabilization of the current deterrence system through arms limitation and disarmament—would be sacrificed for the illusory two in the bush.

The goal of the SDI program does not prove *eo ipso* that the United States takes its global responsibilities as a nuclear superpower lightly. In the joint statement of November 21, 1985, after the summit meeting of President Reagan and General Secretary Gorbachev in Geneva, the Soviet Union also reaffirmed its commitment to "prevent an arms race in space and *terminate it on earth*" (emphasis added).[42] To achieve this goal, the United States will have to bid farewell to the objective of extricating itself from the nuclear dilemma.

Any research, development, and deployment of BMD systems would then, as in the SALT process, be assessed together with the Soviet Union on the basis of their implications for a system of deterrence whose stability would continue to be based on an assured mutual second-strike capability. In this case both sides would, presumably, want to avoid the costly, uncertain, and potentially destabilizing detour via outer space.

Notes

1. Wireless Bulletin from Washington, D.C., Embassy of the United States of America, Bonn (hereafter cited as WB), October 25, 1985, p. 5.

2. *The Strategic Defense Initiative, State Department Fact Sheet,* WB, June 5, 1985, p. 10.

3. Department of Defense, *Report to Congress on the Strategic Defense Initiative,* Washington, D.C., 1985 (hereafter cited as DoD Report), p. 7.

4. Office of Technology Assessment, *Ballistic Missile Defense Technologies,* Washington, D.C., 1985 (hereafter cited as OTA Report), p. 287.

5. "On the other hand, if we had a defensive deterrent—again, hopefully they would never start—but if for some reason, it failed, then very few would get through. Some would. I'm sure some would. But the challenge the president has given us is to find the technologies that will make it so effective out there that only a very few—hopefully, none—would get through" (WB, October 30, 1985, p. 19).

6. Amerika-Dienst, Embassy of the United States of America, *Programm für strategische Verteidigung,* Bonn, April 11, 1984, p. 2 (author's translation).

7. WB, June 5, 1985, p. 5.

8. Fred C. Iklé, *Prepared Statement to the Subcommittee on Strategic and Theater Nuclear Forces of the Senate Armed Services Committee,* WB, February 25, 1985, p. 38; see also his "Nuclear Strategy: Can There Be a Happy Ending?" *Foreign Affairs,* vol. 63, no. 4 (Spring 1985), pp. 810–826.

9. Hans Rühle, "An die Grenzen der Technologie," *Der Spiegel,* no. 48/1985, p. 156.

10. It should be noted, however, that upon the deployment of the submarine-launched Trident II missile, scheduled to begin at the end of the 1980s, the United States will have a weapon whose accuracy reportedly is comparable to that of modern ICBMs and which, together with its ICBMs, will give the United States at least an equivalent counterforce capability.

11. Hearings Before the Subcommittee on the Department of Defense of the Committee on Appropriations, U.S. House of Representatives, *Department of Defense Appropriations for 1986,* Part 7, Washington, D.C., p. 649.

12. George A. Keyworth II, "The Case for Arms Control and the Strategic Defense Initiative," *Arms Control Today,* vol. 15, no. 3 (April 1985), p. 2. Though Abrahamson and Keyworth employ these arguments to support the utility of BMD installations, this does not in any way impair their plausibility in the context considered here. Instead, it only serves to highlight the questionable nature of their argument that a defensive shield is necessary to resolve the ICBM vulnerability problem.

13. This formulation draws upon Kenneth Waltz's argument that "what scenarists imagine seldom has much to do with how governments behave. The bizarre quality of various scenarios that depict a failure of deterrence strengthens one's confidence in it" (Kenneth N. Waltz, *The Spread of Nuclear Weapons: More May Be Better,* Adelphi Papers no. 171 [London: The International Institute for Strategic Studies, 1981], p. 21).

14. WB, June 5, 1985, pp. 8 and 10, respectively.

15. Caspar W. Weinberger, *Soviet Military Power, 1985,* Washington, D.C., 1985, p. 48.

16. *International Herald Tribune,* July 13–14, 1985, p. 3.

17. WB, June 27, 1985, p. 35.

18. DoD Report, p. 23.

19. Cited from OTA Report, Appendix H, p. 298.

20. James Thomson, *Summary Statement,* Hearings Before the Subcommittee on the Department of Defense of the Committee on Appropriations, U.S. House of Representatives, *Department of Defense Appropriations for 1985,* Part 5, Washington, D.C., pp. 934–935.

21. For relevant statements see Appendix H of the OTA Report, p. 302. Secretary Weinberger, on the other hand, considers such concerns to be "unjustified" (cf. WB, November 4, 1985, p. 20).

22. It is difficult, if not impossible, to design a strictly "defensive" weapon because the adversary will assess the potential function of a weapon in the context of the military posture faced. Schelling provides a pertinent example for the importance of the overall context: "Sheltering the population, if shelter is available, is an obviously 'defensive' step if the enemy may launch war before the day is out. It is an equally obvious 'offensive' step if one expects to launch an attack before the day is out and wants to be prepared against counterattack and retaliation" (Thomas C. Schelling, *Arms and Influence* [New Haven and London: Yale University Press, 1966], p. 225). The U.S. debate on the implications of the Soviet civil defense program demonstrates this point. If one assumes that the Soviets want to gain a superior war-fighting capability, shelters can be

interpreted as part of a first-strike strategy because they might be used to limit the damage of a U.S. riposte. Secretary Weinberger, for instance, has discussed the Soviet civil defense program in this context (cf. Hearing Before the Committee on Foreign Relations, U.S. Senate, *U.S. Strategic Doctrine,* December 14, 1982, Washington, D.C., 1983, p. 12).

23. WB, November 22, 1985, p. 4.
24. WB, December 6, 1985, p. 15.
25. WB, December 10, 1985, p. 13.
26. Cf. Harold Brown, "The Strategic Defense Initiative: Defensive Systems and the Strategic Debate," *Survival,* vol. 27, no. 2 (March/April 1985), p. 61.
27. Cf. DoD Report, p. A-7.
28. WB, January 3, 1985, p. 23.
29. Caspar Weinberger, WB, April 12, 1985, p. 23.
30. See *Frankfurter Allgemeine Zeitung,* March 21, 1985, p. 5, and November 29, 1985, p. 3., respectively.
31. Cf. WB, January 3, 1985, p. 23.
32. See Fred Iklé, WB, February 25, 1985, p. 38.
33. Cf., for instance, *International Herald Tribune,* March 6, 1985, p. 1.
34. Soviet Defense Minister Sergei Sokolov has stated that "we would not permit an American monopoly in space" (*Frankfurter Allgemeine Zeitung,* November 1, 1985, p. 2).
35. WB, January 3, 1985, p. 21.
36. WB, January 3, 1985, p. 25.
37. General Abrahamson, for instance, considers a capable offensive to be "important to maintaining deterrence stability as we transition to an offense-defense force balance and new arms control regimes" (WB, April 25, 1985, p. 13).
38. *Time,* November 25, 1985, p. 29.
39. Cf. Department of State and Department of Defense, *Soviet Strategic Defense Programs,* Washington, D.C., 1985, pp. 4 and 5.
40. The United States does not have a spotless record either. The so-called Homing Overlay Experiment of July 1984, in which a modified Minuteman-I ICBM destroyed a dummy warhead outside the atmosphere, strains Article VI(a) of the ABM Treaty under which missiles, other than ABM interceptor missiles, may not be tested in an ABM mode. Cf. James A. Schear, "Arms Control Treaty Compliance," *International Security,* vol. 10, no. 2 (Fall 1985), pp. 176–177.
41. See OTA Report, pp. 267–269, for a discussion of the compatibility of SDI research projects with the ABM Treaty.
42. Department of State Bulletin, vol. 86, no. 2106 (January 1986), p. 8.

8

Strategic Defense and the Future of NATO

Sanford Lakoff

Although President Ronald Reagan's 1983 announcement of the Strategic Defense Initiative caused initial consternation among the leaders of the NATO allies—not least because it came as such a surprise—the project has as yet caused no serious damage to the unity of the alliance. Compared with past crises, including the recent controversy over the deployment of "Euromissiles" (Pershing IIs and land-based cruise missiles), the difficulties over SDI have proven relatively easy to manage. Great Britain and the Federal Republic of Germany have agreed to cooperate actively in the research, and the United States has given its blessing, however warily, to the French-sponsored EUREKA project, designed as a civilian technological alternative to SDI that would keep the western European nations from falling further behind the United States should the U.S. high-technology industry be disproportionately benefited by SDI-sponsored research. Despite Soviet efforts to depict development of space strike weapons as the critical obstacle to East-West accord, Europeans have not responded strongly enough to revive the campaign for nuclear disarmament or to force the question toward the center of parliamentary and party politics.

There are at least two reasons why SDI has not provoked a serious crisis in NATO, both of which indicate that it remains a potentially explosive issue despite what has happened so far. One is that the project is still largely a matter for laboratory research. As a result, discussions of possible deployments and strategic and political consequences remain highly speculative. Unlike the Euromissiles, SDI is not an actual weapons

---

Prepared under a grant from the Carnegie Corporation of New York.

system to be immediately deployed, whether on European soil or in space above Western Europe. To the extent that it offers access to U.S. research funding without requiring any commitment to deployment, SDI represents something for nothing at a time when governments are hard pressed to find resources for research and development. West European leaders and their cabinets can afford to suppress any doubts they may have about the feasibility or the advisability of actual deployment in favor of maintaining NATO solidarity and good relations with Washington. To opt out at this stage would only increase the temptation for the United States to concentate its efforts on a defense of the North American continent instead of also taking into account the different defensive requirements for Europe. It could also tempt the Reagan administration to join with congressional forces pressing for disengagement from Europe. SDI, moreover, has become a subject for a kind of linkage in U.S.-European relations over defense procurement. Rightly or wrongly, defense officials apparently feared that if they balked at joining SDI, the United States might retaliate by denying European bids for other important defense contracts.

The other reason SDI has so far not been more of a source of discord is that the Soviet effort to portray it as the greatest obstacle to a renewal of détente has been vitiated by the behavior of the Soviets themselves. Despite the steadfast refusal of the United States to bargain over SDI, the Soviets have returned to the negotiations. By contrast, the emplacement of Euromissiles resulted in a Soviet walkout from both the INF negotiations and the Strategic Arms Reduction Talks (START). European leaders have been assured by spokesmen for the Reagan administration that because SDI is a research project, to be conducted within the limits of the ABM Treaty, it need not jeopardize existing arms control agreements or preclude agreements to reduce strategic and tactical nuclear weapons. Indeed, such agreements are considered desirable as a first step toward the "defense transition" that SDI research is designed to make possible. Europeans may harbor serious doubts (as do domestic U.S. critics) as to whether certain of the tests contemplated under SDI are in fact permissible under the ABM Treaty, and they may fear that President Reagan's commitment to the project may prevent him from making compromises that may be necessary to obtain arms reduction, but for the time being they can take satisfaction from the apparent success of the 1985 Geneva summit and hope that it will lead to more substantive agreement.

Both issues are potentially dangerous to NATO unity, however. If the research effort shows that some types of defensive systems are feasible, there could well be pressure to deploy them. If that happens, controversy over their possible strategic and political effects would become more acute and quite possibly divisive.

Among the portents of difficulties to come were the doubts expressed by two official European spokesmen. The British Foreign Secretary, Sir Geoffrey Howe, observed that "from a purely European standpoint it has yet to be demonstrated why a mixed offensive-defensive strategy would be better for European security than, for example, a strengthened ABM Treaty and deep cuts in strategic offensive arms."[1] Hans Rühle, director of the Planning Staff in the FRG's Ministry of Defense, stated the European concern even more explicitly.

> Should, as may be assumed, both superpowers follow the road charted by Reagan, their territories would become invulnerable sanctuaries, while Europe, even if it deployed a corresponding defense system, would be rid of few of its security policy concerns. Although in such a case protection from the Soviet ballistic missiles, e.g., the SS-20 [would be] . . . guaranteed, Soviet cruise missiles, short-range missiles, and low-flying bombers could not be prevented from penetrating into Western Europe. What is worse, all conventional arms systems would regain in importance, recalling pre-nuclear times—not a particularly pleasant perspective in view of the existing conventional imbalance in favor of the Soviet Union.[2]

In the short term, if arms reduction negotiations are not successful, and SDI is held responsible, European opinion could become aroused and NATO governments might be compelled to reconsider their willingness to cooperate even on the basis that the program is devoted only to research. General Secretary Mikhail Gorbachev's bold diplomatic stroke in January 1986, proposing the total elimination of nuclear weapons by the end of the century by negotiation, may have been intended largely for propaganda effect, but it could well represent a seductive alternative to SDI for many Europeans who are apt to be more anxious for détente than is the present U.S. leadership.

In order to address the potential problems that SDI poses for the future of NATO, it is necessary to appreciate in the first place how difficult it has been during the past forty years to establish and maintain the unity of the Western alliance in the face of conflicting national interests and ideological differences. One of the critical problems is that the United States is the leader of a global alliance with global interests and responsibilities. The primary concern of the European allies is with the European dimension of the East-West conflict. Europeans are bound to be reluctant to exacerbate tensions in Europe for the sake of U.S. interests and commitments elsewhere, and they are bound to be tempted to accept opportunities to defuse tensions in Europe by improving relations with the nations of the Soviet bloc even though such improvements may not affect Soviet behavior elsewhere and may weaken the unity of NATO. As Earl Ravenal pointed out in an essay on NATO, the conflict of perspectives becomes most salient in matters of strategy.

> The alliance of Atlantic nations, in its history, has been beset by many kinds of problems. There have been the periodic recrudescence of commercial and agricultural disputes; the irreconcilable antagonisms of pairs of nations, such as Greece and Turkey; the threat of Eurocommunism; the acrimony revolving around burden-sharing; the complaints about the 'one-way street' of American military production for the alliance; the assaults of neutralists and anti-American political groups; the failure of 'consultation' and the recriminations about American 'hegemony.' But whatever else is wrong with the Atlantic alliance, its essential problems are strategic. The relationships that constitute the very structure of the international system are strategic (though, of course, other functions, such as economic situations and assets, can be adopted as implements of strategy). In NATO the principal problem is that the United States and Europe have persistently failed to resolve their discordant strategic conceptions.[3]

It is precisely because SDI poses a stark choice between strategic conceptions that it arouses misgivings in Europe. As observed in a committee report for the most recent annual meeting of the North Atlantic Assembly, "There is a real danger of a transatlantic crisis brought about by a conflict of nuclear philosophies." The reason, the rapporteur noted, was concern over whether NATO should continue to try to strengthen its ability to deter attack by means of nuclear and conventional offense or commit itself to moving toward greater and greater reliance on defensive measures.[4]

The strategic issue is embedded, however, in a broader context of political concerns and sensitivities. A review of initial European reactions is therefore a useful essential foundation for considering the prospective impact of SDI on relations between the United States and its European allies.

The Initial Reaction in Western Europe

In Western Europe, the president's initiative aroused both apprehension and anxiety. The reasons overlap and are held with greater or lesser intensity by different governments.

1. *The decision was made unilaterally, without prior consultation.* Although this was hardly the first instance of a unilateral U.S. shift in strategic thinking with important consequences for NATO, there was already concern over what the British strategist Michael Howard has described

as "the degree to which the Europeans have abandoned the primary responsibility for their defense to the United States."[5] If domestic critics could complain that the decision was made from the top down, without adequate preparation—so much so that it took the weapons specialists in the Pentagon by surprise—this criticism was felt all the more strongly in Europe. It was particularly rankling or threatening because it came at a time when prominent Americans were calling on Europeans to take more of a role in their own defense. The logical interpretation some Europeans put on the president's message was that it was intended as much as a signal to them as to the Soviets—a signal that the United States was determined to concern itself with its own defense regardless of what its allies chose to do on behalf of theirs, and perhaps that the United States was tired of trying to maintain allied unity without much response to its repeated request for a more equitable sharing of the burden.

2. *The president's proposal seemed to augur a fundamental change in NATO strategic doctrine.* That doctrine had already been altered, from simple deterrence to massive retaliation and from massive retaliation to flexible response, but this change looked as though it would be far more basic because all the others presupposed a strategy of deterrence by the threat of nuclear and conventional retaliation. It was not clear, however, that the president actually had in mind such a fundamental shift of strategic doctrine or that, if he did, it was really conceivable. Nevertheless, the proposal of SDI implied that a fundamental shift was in the offing.

3. *Because of the hostile Soviet reaction, the president's initiative seemed to diminish prospects for a resumption of serious arms control negotiations between East and West.* As the Pentagon in particular insisted that SDI was not a bargaining chip, these fears intensified. Although Europeans depend on the U.S. military shield and are therefore anxious not to allow the Soviets to split the alliance, they are more concerned than the United States with decreasing tensions between East and West through arms control, thereby reducing the danger of a war that would most likely begin on European soil. Insofar as SDI seemed to make those negotiations more difficult, or perhaps to threaten the whole process of arms control by triggering an arms race that was both offensive and defensive, Europeans were bound to be disturbed by the uncertainties created by Reagan's proposal. The argument reported to have taken place within the administration—in which National Security Adviser Robert C. McFarlane argued that the ABM Treaty should be interpreted to allow virtually whatever development and testing the United States decided was necessary—only fueled these fears even though the president is said to have settled the issue by supporting the somewhat more restrictive reading made by the State Department. Secretary Weinberger's

letter, leaked on the eve of the summit, urging the president not to agree to any limitations on SDI research not required by the treaty (even as liberally interpreted by the State Department) only rekindled this particular anxiety. And the fact that the summit produced no agreement even on a framework of principles, but only reiteration of the previous positions of both parties, seemed to justify this earlier skepticism.

4. *During a "defense transition," crisis instability would increase.* Assuming that the Soviets were indeed technologically inferior to the United States in these relatively exotic technologies, the United States could be expected to achieve a more or less effective defense before the Soviet Union could deploy a system of its own. During a crisis, the Soviets might be tempted to stage a preemptive strike before their offensive forces could be degraded by a U.S. deployment. Alternatively, if the United States should deploy a defense before the Soviets were capable of overcoming it, or before they had succeeded in erecting one of their own, the United States might be tempted to strike without suffering catastrophic damage.[6] In any event, neither side could remain confident of its ability to respond with devastating force in a crisis, and insofar as this capacity had promoted crisis stability, such stability would not be assured in the future.

5. *Deployment of even modest defenses by the United States would lead to a breakdown of the ABM Treaty regime, and the comparable deployment of defenses by the Soviet Union would degrade the British and French independent deterrents.* Even though Soviet defenses might not be able to thwart a full-scale attack by the United States, they could be effective enough to contain or nullify the independent British and French deterrent, despite the efforts now under way to add penetration aids to these systems. Thus, the unilateral U.S. initiative seemed to undercut French and British strategy, whether or not by design and regardless of whether it could ultimately succeed.

6. *Extended deterrence might not remain meaningful in conditions in which deterrence was expected to function by means of defense.* The threat facing Europe was from short-range missiles and air-breathing weapons, which could reach their targets in much shorter time than the 30 minutes needed for ICBMs (coupled with the additional warning time that might be provided by detection of preparations to launch). The launch of depressed-trajectory weapons against European targets, along with the use of intermediate-range missiles, would deprive Europeans of any comparable warning, and these weapons could not easily be intercepted by the systems proposed for SDI. The threat to Europe would have to be met by the development of anti-tactical ABM systems, which were not a prominent part of SDI as originally proposed, and which might

be even less likely to provide a leakproof shield than the layered defense proposed for SDI.

7. *The specter of decoupling: By making the dangers faced by the U.S. population less than those faced by Europeans, the likelihood that Americans would feel bound to come to the defense of Europe would disappear.* Why should Americans be willing to become involved in the defense of Europe if they felt safe in "Fortress America"? If Henry Kissinger and others had been right earlier in warning their NATO allies that they should not expect the United States to undertake measures that would be suicidal, and therefore incredible, how much less likely would the United States be to come to Europe's side if the United States succeeded in erecting a nuclear shield over itself? The strength of the alliance, Christoph Bertram remarked, had come from the sharing of risk.[7] And if the United States and the USSR should both deploy effective defenses, the likelihood would be that "Europe would be doomed to the kind of conventional war, or of 'limited' war, that has been its nightmare and that extended nuclear deterrence was intended to prevent," as Stanley Hoffman put it.[8]

8. *U.S. subvention of its high-technology industry would confront Europe with another "American challenge" in civilian economic terms.* French President François Mitterand gave voice to these fears when he complained that Europeans would be allowed to cooperate only as subcontractors. West German officials worried that U.S. sensitivity over the security of high technology would prevent full-scale transfer of new technology to its European allies. Richard Perle's warnings about the dangers of industrial espionage did not allay these misgivings.[9] The economic consideration, however, has been two-edged. Britain was reluctant to break ranks with the United States partly because of fear of being deprived of other possible military contracts and partly because of a more positive desire to obtain guarantees for at least a fraction of the research effort. Similarly, West German firms were willing to consider participating, especially after their representatives were reassured that the United States looked forward to full-scale cooperation unhindered by security considerations. The French, however, took a very different view, seizing the opportunity to launch EUREKA. This project has so far met with remarkably widespread acceptance and could well become a major rival, even though the United States insists that it would complement rather than oppose the aims of SDI.

These anxieties had an initial effect when President Reagan came under pressure from domestic agencies to accept a broad interpretation of what was permitted under the ABM Treaty. Prime Minister Margaret Thatcher's flight to Washington was reminiscent of Clement Attlee's when the United States was considering the use of atomic bombs in the

Korean War. Thatcher's need to convince the president to make clear that SDI would not jeopardize the ABM Treaty and that the United States would consider deployment only after consultation with European allies, was an indication of the difficulties resulting from the unilateral character of the decision and the greater level of concern in Europe over the impact of SDI on East-West relations.

The Impact on East-West Relations

The impact of SDI on East-West relations is disputed. Supporters of the president's program claim that it brought the Soviets back to the bargaining table at Geneva and will eventually compel them to recognize that they too must place greater emphasis on defensive rather than offensive weapons. Opponents argue that the Soviets agreed to resume negotiations because their effort to drive a wedge between the United States and its European allies over the deployment of INF weapons had failed and because they saw in SDI an opportunity to seize the propaganda initiative again by accusing the United States of attempting to militarize space and of jeopardizing the existing arms control treaties. In any case, opponents argue, the president's refusal to construe SDI as a bargaining chip will lead the Soviets to resist agreement for further reductions of offensive arms and will in the end only exacerbate the arms race.

Which of these interpretations of the future of arms control proves correct will depend to a considerable degree on the willingness of both sides to strike a bargain. The Soviets probably want some sort of bargain because of a general interest in the revival of détente, but only if they can prevent a full-scale U.S. effort to achieve strategic superiority. This general interest reflects the priority General Secretary Gorbachev has placed on a modernization of the Soviet economy. In order to accomplish this modernization, he needs to be able to control his budget so that he does not have to divert funds into military research likely to have relatively little civilian payoff. The United States can afford this sort of diversion better than the Soviets can, especially because the United States can benefit more from spinoffs in computers, for example, than can the Soviet Union. A third-generation computer of value in SDI will be of great benefit to U.S. industry, which is ready for it, but Soviet needs are more elementary. If he chooses to emphasize countermeasures, Gorbachev may have none of these benefits, though his costs will be correspondingly lower. In addition, the Soviets need access to Western technology and financial credits in order to achieve these economic goals. Continued difficulty in East-West relations will pose a serious obstacle to the development of favorable trade relations not only with the United States and Western Europe but also with Japan. Although the Soviets have potential diplomatic bargaining leverage with Japan in the form of occupied northern territories of Japan, Tokyo would be most unlikely to risk a serious rupture in its relationship with the United States, and the Soviets are just as unlikely to relinquish their control of these territories.

Soviet opposition to SDI on the grounds that it represents a militarization of space is in some respects a disingenuous protest and in others an honest recognition that the U.S. program poses a significant potential threat. Space has already been militarized in principle by both sides. Some 80 percent of the Soviet space systems launched in the past year have been of a military character. These consist of military support systems that provide surveillance, communication, and navigation assistance and of electronic ocean reconnaissance (EORSAT) and radar ocean reconnaissance (RORSAT) satellites, which could make possible "real-time" targeting coordination.[10] The U.S. program, the Soviets argue, is a new departure because it would put in space lethal weapons that might be used for offensive rather than defensive missions. These they refer to as space strike weapons.

In fact, there is some possibility that space-based weapons could strike at "soft" ground targets other than rocket boosters, though at present the prospect is still speculative and is not the primary goal of SDI. A more likely offensive use of space-based defensive systems would be to threaten satellites, and much of the research on SDI overlaps with development of anti-satellite weapons. Conceivably, a U.S. superiority in space-based weapons could be used offensively against Soviet satellites. Conceivably, too, if either side develops an effective system before the other, that side would acquire an offensive advantage because it would theoretically be able to launch a first strike with confidence that its system, even though it might not be leakproof against a full-scale offense, would be able to absorb a "ragged second strike."

The Soviet criticism of SDI masks the fact that the USSR itself has made heavy investments in defense, both in deployment and in advanced research. The Soviets have the only deployed ABM system ringing Moscow, and they are reportedly upgrading this system so that it will not only be silo-based, but will possess both endo- and exo-atmospheric interception capability, thus giving it two of the layers of a multi-layered defense. In addition, the Soviets have deployed a thick anti-aircraft shield throughout the country, one that is designed to intercept aircraft—which carry more than half the megatonnage currently in the U.S. arsenal. The Soviets have also tested and presumably could deploy a ground-based ASAT, which could be used to blind some U.S. satellites in the event of hostilities.

At the Geneva summit, the Soviets reiterated their view that SDI represents an effort to achieve space strike weapons, and they insisted that U.S. pursuit of the program would rule out any agreement to reduce offensive weapons. Their offer of such a reduction was contingent on U.S. willingness to abandon SDI. There is an important ambiguity in the Soviet position, however. Although prior to the summit Soviet spokesmen in the arms control negotiations said that the Soviet position was that all research on SDI had to be renounced because the intention was to develop the weapons, elsewhere they have acknowledged that laboratory research is not forbidden under the ABM Treaty and have said that their aim is to win U.S. agreement not to test and develop such systems.

The issue then boils down to whether the United States is willing to accept agreed restraints on SDI research that can meet Soviet objections. The U.S. position is that it will abide by a restrictive interpretation of the ABM Treaty, but the Reagan administration's notion of what such a restriction entails is controversial. Much depends on whether the tests the SDI office intends to conduct are considered tests of "components" or "sub-components" (or "adjuncts"). The treaty language is ambiguous in indicating what such terms mean, and the administration's restrictive interpretation would allow for tests that critics—including the chief negotiator of the treaty for the United States—say stretch the meaning of the treaty language beyond what was intended.[11] In a treaty negotiation, it is conceivable that the United States might agree to submit certain of these issues to clarification within the Standing Consultative Commission or might agree to postpone such tests indefinitely in exchange for a favorable response to U.S. arms reductions proposals.

Both sides experience pressure to produce something from arms control negotiations. It is hard to see what could be accomplished in connection with strategic offensive weapons if there is no agreement on SDI research. But this pressure should not be discounted, especially because some of it comes from the U.S. Congress, where sentiment in favor of SDI is not as high as it is in the Pentagon or, for that matter, in public opinion. Especially among the Democrats, who constitute a majority of the members of the House of Representatives, there is concern that the vast expenditures contemplated for SDI would be wasteful and need to be controlled in view of the budget deficit. Democrats are also concerned that this project is too speculative to allow it to block arms reduction agreements. The congressional insistence on limiting deployments of the MX missile and the refusal to authorize further tests of the ASAT are straws in the wind. Unless the president can report further progress in arms reduction talks, his requests for support of SDI, which have already been reduced considerably in Congress, could run into even more serious resistance. And the same political forces that made such headway with the freeze campaign, and whose thunder the president may have successfully stolen with his announcement of SDI, could return to the hustings with even greater effect if the talks are stalled.

There is less pressure on the Soviets to reach an arms reduction agreement, except insofar as the failure of an effort to renew détente could be costly in terms of trade relations with the West. Although the administration may complain that congressional resistance to SDI and ASAT testing weaken its bargaining power in Geneva, the most important leverage on the Soviets is probably good economic relations.

It is quite possible, however, that these talks will get nowhere. In that case, the best that could be expected is that the regime of SALT II would continue in force but no further progress would be achieved. In such an atmosphere, the ABM Treaty might gradually become a dead letter as both sides continue with efforts to develop systems that exploit its loopholes—in the first place to develop ASAT weapons, in the second to develop anti-tactical ballistic missiles (ATBMs).

The Soviets have explicitly warned the countries of Western Europe that they will regard their participation in the SDI effort as an unfriendly act, and they could conceivably retaliate by refusing to allow East Germany to improve relations with the Federal Republic. This effort seems unlikely to have much success. The Soviets have also pointed out that the ABM Treaty contains a provision barring either signatory from exchanging information on ABM systems with a third party. This would appear to prevent cooperation on anti-tactical systems, but this objection can be overridden by the same legal interpretations that have been used to permit testing of new sub-components. Because the technology needed for an ATBM is not precisely the same as that for an ABM, it is presumably possible for cooperation to take place without violating the terms of the treaty. The Europeans may embark on their own ATBM SDI so as to avoid borrowing U.S. technology. For the time being, the Soviet effort to make SDI a substitute for the cruise missile is not likely to have great success—especially because at this stage SDI is very much a research program, unlike the cruise missile and Pershing II, which involved deployments on European soil. If the Soviets went so far as to break off negotiations because of SDI, however, and if they carried through on their threat to declare the ABM Treaty null and void and to build more offensive weapons, thus effectively tearing up SALT I and SALT II, the effect on European public opinion could be far more serious.

Consequences for the NATO Alliance

The longer-term consequences for the alliance are also uncertain. If SDI should succeed in producing an effective shield against nuclear weapons, both long-range and short-range, it would certainly revolutionize strategy by putting in question the principle of deterrence by retaliation on which Western strategy has been based. If the Soviets should develop such a technology simultaneously, it is conceivable that the way would again be open for conventional warfare as some critics of SDI have charged; this of course would have grave consequences for Europe. However, there are few qualified scientists who consider a truly effective defense within the realm of possibility. Most agree that a more likely technical possibility would be the development of an effective hard-point defense system, relying both on terminal interception and on some mid-course and boost-phase systems. For such a system, the technological gap between the United States and Soviet Union is not as significant as for the far more demanding defense envisioned by the president. Nor would such a deployment immediately upset the present strategic reliance on deterrence by threat of retaliation. It would serve mainly to protect the land-based leg of the deterrent. This leg happens to be of more relative importance to the Soviet Union than to the United States because the United States relies more heavily on submarines and on the promise of a new stealth technology. The Soviets, however, have lately emphasized the need to develop mobile missiles as a way of making their land-based missiles less vulnerable to increasingly accurate U.S. SLBMs and possibly also the MX and stealth bombers and cruise missiles. Soviet willingness to limit deployment of mobile missiles could be linked to an agreement to allow more ground-based terminal defense than envisioned in the ABM Treaty.

Under these circumstances, the possibility might be opened up for a revision of the ABM Treaty to allow for increased deployment of ground-based systems (with some airborne and possibly space-based detection facilities) in conjunction with agreed reductions of offensive arms. Such a scheme has been proposed under the heading of a "defense-protected build-down."[12] Although there appear to be insuperable difficulties in calculating the precise exchange ratios of defensive and offensive weapons that this scheme in its purest form envisions, it may be possible to develop a broad notion of asymmetrical equivalence more or less along the lines of previous arms control agreements. Thus, the United States and the Soviet Union might both be permitted to deploy defenses of hard-point fixed targets, or possibly of missile fields in which mobility would be permitted, while accepting constraints on the deployment of offensive ground-based weapons and of other weapons that are considered necessary because they are relatively invulnerable to preemptive strikes. If defenses could enhance invulnerability, the present degree of redundancy would become less necessary.

Conclusion

If the current round of negotiations produces no tangible results the alliance will suffer a considerable strain. The strain can be avoided if the U.S. program proceeds at a moderate pace and if an agreement is worked out to permit both sides to deploy certain defensive systems as a way of reassuring both of the reliability of the deterrent. This could have unequal results, however, allowing the Soviets to protect somewhat more of their civilian population than the United States would be allowed.[13]

If advances in technology should one day make possible a shield against nuclear weapons, there would be no way short of total nuclear disarmament to inhibit either the development or the deployment of such a system. Nor should there be any reason to do so, because reliance on the threat of retaliation poses serious moral problems as well as the danger of accident and escalation of more limited conventional conflicts. A more likely route to the reduction and virtual elimination of strategic nuclear weapons is the maintenance of superpower cooperation in the effort to manage the arms race. If there is such cooperation, the first stages of a defense transition can be undertaken on terms that do not threaten to give either side an offensive advantage. Further steps will require far more active cooperation, but they may become impossible as a practical matter unless the first steps are taken now.

As for tactical weapons, unless both sides are prepared to abandon offensive weapons in the European theater altogether, there is probably no way to halt research on defenses against such weapons. In view of the possibilities of salvage-fusing short-range weapons, however, it hardly seems likely that a fully effective defense against such weapons will be possible. Given the technical difficulties, the surest path to the removal of the nuclear threat in Europe appears to be the negotiation of political records aimed at defusing tensions.

The conclusion seems inescapable that although, for the time being, the potential conflict between European concerns and the latest U.S. strategic initiative has been averted, that conflict would become acute if the United States were to move to development and deployment of strategic defense outside the context of a general offensive and defensive arms control agreement with the Soviet Union. The conflict will not reach such a climax, however, if the research now under way does not live up to optimistic expectations or if domestic pressures within the

United States, such as opposition to projected high levels of expenditure for SDI from congressional critics or other parts of the defense establishment, reduce the momentum of the effort. A gradual and partial "defense transition," which would add some defenses to protect the deterrent force—an outcome that is not at all the one President Reagan had in mind in his 1983 address—would pose no significant challenge to the strategic assumptions on which NATO has come to depend. In view of the formidable technical challenges that must be overcome if SDI is to fulfill the president's vision of a world set free from the threat of nuclear weapons, the more likely prospect is that the program will have far less radical effects. For the foreseeable future, therefore, the unity of NATO will probably not be seriously threatened by SDI.

Notes

1. Quoted in "Interim Report of Special Committee on Nuclear Weapons," North Atlantic Assembly (San Francisco, Calif., October 1985), p. 15.
2. Quoted in "General Report of the Scientific and Technical Committee," North Atlantic Assembly (November 1984), p. 27.
3. Earl C. Ravenal, *NATO: The Tides of Discontent*. Policy Papers in International Affairs no. 23 (Berkeley, Calif.: Institute of International Studies, 1985), p. 5.
4. "Interim Report of Special Committee on Nuclear Weapons," North Atlantic Assembly (San Francisco, Calif., October 1985), p. 9.
5. Michael Howard, "Deterrence, Consensus and Reassurance in the Defense of Europe," *Defense and Consensus: The Domestic Aspects of Western Security* Adelphi Papers no. 184 (London: The International Institute for Strategic Studies, 1983), p. 23.
6. This scenario was outlined by the Soviet leader, Yuri Andropov, in response to President Reagan's 1983 address. It is discussed sympathetically in McGeorge Bundy, George F. Kennan, Robert S. McNamara, and Gerard Smith, "The President's Choice: Star Wars or Arms Control," *Foreign Affairs*, 63, 2 (Winter 1984/85), pp. 270-271.
7. Christoph Bertram, "Strategic Defense and the Western Alliance," *Daedalus*, 114, 3 (Summer 1985), p. 293.
8. Stanley Hoffmann, "The U.S. and Western Europe: Wait and Worry," *Foreign Affairs*, 63, 3 (1984), p. 639.
9. Perle is reported to have said in May 1985 that the United States would not share SDI technology completely with its allies but would decide to do so on a case-by-case basis. See "Interim Report, Sub-Committee on Defense Cooperation, Military Committee," North Atlantic Assembly (San Francisco, Calif., October 1985), p. 5.
10. The Soviet defense program is described in Department of Defense, *Report to Congress on the Strategic Defense Initiative* (Washington, D.C.: De-

partment of Defense, 1985), appendix C-3; and *Soviet Military Power 1985* (Washington, D.C.: Department of Defense, 1984).

11. See Alan B. Sherr, *Legal Issues of the "Star Wars" Defense Program* (Boston, Mass.: The Lawyers Alliance for Nuclear Arms Control, Inc., June 1984); and Thomas K. Longstreth, John E. Pike, and John B. Rhinelander, *The Impact of the U.S. and Soviet Ballistic Missile Defense Programs on the ABM Treaty* (Washington, D.C.: National Campaign to Save the ABM Treaty, March 1985).

12. Alvin N. Weinberg and Jack N. Barkenbus, "Stabilizing Star Wars," *Foreign Policy*, 54 (Spring 1984), pp. 164–170.

13. See Coit D. Blacker, "Defending Missiles, Not People: Hard-Site Defense," *Issues in Science and Technology*, 2, 1 (Fall 1985), p. 42.

9

SDI: Strategic Disengagement and Independence

Wolfram F. Hanrieder

In the 1970s the tentative and modest steps toward arms control embodied in the first and second Strategic Arms Limitation Talks (SALT I and SALT II) were accompanied and sustained by an East-West understanding that it was in the common interest to stabilize and legitimize the European territorial and political status quo. Stabilization of the arms race and stabilization of the European status quo were the twin pillars on which the détente process of the early and middle 1970s rested.[1] Considerations of this nature also explain the reluctance of the first Reagan administration to engage in serious arms control negotiations. Washington showed little interest in reviving a process of détente, thus depriving arms control of a supportive political context; and it perceived the United States—accurately or not—as having fallen behind in the arms race with the Soviet Union. As George Ball noted,

> President Reagan's logic leads to a negation of arms control. If America is in the lead with respect to any new weapons, we should not give up that advantage by agreeing to outlaw or limit that system, but should instead push forcefully ahead. If, on the other hand, we are behind the Soviets in some new generation of weapons, we should reject any limitation until we have caught up and surpassed our adversary.[2]

Nuclear Stability and Alliance Management: Deterrence and Reassurance

Throughout the thirty-five year history of the North Atlantic Treaty Organization, the central military doctrine that governed all aspects of Western security policy was that of strategic deterrence, which served as the military-strategic implementation of the overarching U.S. political strategy of containment. Containment and deterrence were mutually reinforcing elements of U.S. global strategy that faced, at the divide of Europe, toward both East and West. The strategy was intended to check the Soviet Union at the same time that it established in Western Europe, above all in the Federal Republic of Germany, the geopolitical base on which the U.S. cold war effort could be securely emplaced. Just as containment embodied a dual component—one directed toward the Soviet Union, the other toward the Federal Republic—so did deterrence. While one component of U.S. deterrence policy was aimed at the Soviet Union, threatening dire consequences in case of Soviet aggression, an equally important element was aimed at U.S. allies in Western Europe, reassuring them that their security interests were adequately accommodated by the first component. Together, the threat of punishing the opponent and its attendant reassuring effect on the alliance made up the core of the transatlantic security partnership and underlined the determination of the United States to contain the Soviet Union and protect Western Europe.[3]

Over the decades, the deterring and the reassuring aspects of Western strategy (and the various doctrinal announcements that sought to serve both purposes) became much less complementary. The gradual weakening of U.S. strategic superiority vis-à-vis the Soviet Union brought with it the gradual weakening of West European confidence that the United States would risk national nuclear suicide for the sake of the alliance. As the Soviet Union began to reach nuclear parity with the United States and as the idea of extended deterrence became less convincing, the principles of deterrence and reassurance—on whose complementarity the common purpose and cohesion of the Atlantic security community ultimately rested—began to diverge.

This created a dilemma for which neither the United States nor the Europeans could be blamed and from which they could not escape. Nuclear parity between the two superpowers led to conflicts of interest between the United States—which now needed to delay or otherwise qualify the use of nuclear weapons—and NATO partners at the forward line of defense, such as the FRG, who were prohibited from obtaining a national nuclear capability but could not accept a strategy that implied sustained conventional warfare at the expense of their territories and populations. The central dilemma of NATO [during the last decade and a half] could not be resolved: The United States, in seeking to limit the arms race and arrive at a stable nuclear balance, was compelled to deal with the Soviet Union on the basis of *parity*, as was reflected in the arrangements of SALT. At the same time, Washington could not convincingly guarantee the security of Western Europe except on the basis of an implied U.S. nuclear *superiority*. As a consequence, West

Germany's initial misgivings about NATO's doctrine of flexible response were increased by the advent of U.S.-Soviet nuclear parity. The West Germans feared that deterrence would be weakened by the U.S. inclination to avoid or postpone nuclear intervention; that the idea of flexible response would add to the Warsaw Pact's geographical advantage with respect to deployment and resupply; and, most insidious, that the thinking behind flexible response implied the "divisibility" of deterrence, that Europe would become a battlefield while the United States remained a sanctuary.

All this brought into sharp focus the central paradox in the West European, and especially the West German, attitude toward their nuclear protector: They seemed equally afraid that the United States would use nuclear weapons and that it would not. The West Europeans feared, in equal measure, lack of U.S. circumspection and lack of U.S. resolve; they worried (especially during the Reagan administration) about the global confrontation with the Soviet Union that Washington seemed to favor, but they also feared the possibility of U.S. unilateralism and disengagement from Europe. Were it not for the fact that the Soviet Union, for its part, has been unable to fashion a sophisticated European policy—above all, in its apparent inability to define its security in terms other than military—the transatlantic connection would be even weaker than it already is. At any rate, it might be worthwhile for U.S. diplomacy to consider that confidence-building measures should be addressed to allies as well as to opponents; and that the widening gap between deterrence and reassurance can be narrowed only by an appropriately circumspect and measured U.S. diplomacy, coupled with a correspondingly plausible arms control strategy.

The Reagan Administration's "Credibility" Gap

A major burden was placed on U.S.–West German relations during the first Reagan administration because the president found it extremely difficult to persuade his West European allies that he was seriously committed to arms control. The Geneva talks on intermediate-range nuclear forces (INF) commenced ten months into the president's term and then, it seemed, only at the insistence of the U.S. Congress and of European leaders who were themselves pressed by expressions of public concern over the impending deployment of Pershing II and cruise missiles. The Geneva talks on strategic arms reduction (START) began seventeen months after President Reagan took office, again only after extensive expressions of concern over the delay, in the United States as well as abroad. The administration placed known opponents of the SALT II treaty in key positions in its arms control agencies and negotiating teams and, even so, felt obliged to force the resignation of the director of the Arms Control and Disarmament Agency for being "overzealous." The president postponed indefinitely the negotiations on a comprehensive test ban treaty, arguing the need for more nuclear testing, even though these talks had been supported by every president since Dwight D. Eisenhower.

Most disturbing of all, perhaps, the administration raised discussions about "protracted" nuclear war and U.S. determination to prevail in such a war; there was a nagging suspicion in Europe, fueled by injudicious U.S. statements, that Washington aimed for nuclear superiority over the Soviet Union and that the deployment of missiles capable of reaching the Soviet Union from Western Europe was one way of fulfilling that intention.[4] Moreover, the Reagan administration's anti-Soviet rhetoric and its black-and-white view of the East-West contest called into question the substance as well as style of U.S. diplomacy. The failure of the Reagan administration to develop an attitude (not to speak of a policy) toward the Soviet Union that conveyed anything but confrontational hostility placed severe strains on the transatlantic alliance. Many West Europeans were determined to compensate for the lack of a constructive U.S. policy with one of their own, with the somewhat ironic result that they appeared more confident than their distant and secure transatlantic partner of being able to deal with the Soviet Union through diplomatic and political means.

Most significant perhaps, it appeared as if there were no longer agreement among the Western powers over the nature and intensity of the Soviet threat—one of the most fundamental issues that NATO needs to address and yet avoids. In part, no doubt, these differing assessments derived from the differing views provided by global and regional political perspectives: Washington sees itself challenged by Moscow everywhere and on everything (especially when the president views the global East-West contest as a zero-sum game between the United States and the Soviet Union); the Europeans take a more limited view of the Soviet threat. But the differing views of the Soviet Union cannot be explained by global and regional perspectives alone. It is difficult at times to avoid the impression that both nuclear superpowers seek to exploit their nuclear-strategic preponderance to compensate for diplomatic, political, and even economic infirmities and to exploit their nuclear status for purposes of alliance management.

The militarization of diplomacy is especially debilitating for the Federal Republic of Germany. NATO has contracted to an essentially bilateral security arrangement between the United States and the FRG; and the FRG is especially dependent on its transatlantic security partner. As a consequence, Washington's political use of military-strategic matters and arms control arrangements has had a profound effect on the limits and possibilities of West German diplomacy. Increased nuclear saturation of both German states has tied their governments even closer to their respective superpower protectors and to their respective views of the East-West conflict; it has emphasized the division of Europe and of Germany and has stood in the way of mapping more constructive ways to ease that division; and it has narrowed the range of East-West European diplomacy and supported the essentially conservative European policy pursued by both the United States and the Soviet Union.

The Devolution of Extended Deterrence

Extended deterrence—the U.S. commitment to initiate nuclear war for the sake of an ally—has been the backbone of the transatlantic security compact and the enshrined nuclear-strategic doctrine of NATO. Even though its credibility has become impaired over the decades, and even though its doctrinal purity has become qualified with the principles of flexible response, extended deterrence remains the political symbol of the indivisibility of the Western defense effort and of the willingness to share alliance benefits and risks in equal measure. In short, extended deterrence has become, at least in part, a fiction—an alliance myth that has to be protected from the rough and unpalatable realities of the East-West nuclear balance and the inevitable reconsiderations of U.S. national interests that these realities bring with them.

Even myths are challenged, however. Henry Kissinger's much-noted Brussels speech of September 1979 and the famous article by the "gang of four" in *Foreign Affairs* are two of the most prominent examples.[5] But there was a certain avuncular quality about these arguments: They were friendly in their intentions toward Europe, basically unquestioning of the continuing political centrality for the United States of the U.S.-European connection, and perhaps even somewhat patronizing in their underlying theme of "how to save the Europeans from themselves." But there also developed a school of U.S. nuclear-strategic "realists," well represented in the Pentagon, who were equally concerned with the shrinking validity of the U.S. nuclear commitment to Europe, but under the motto of "how to save ourselves from the Europeans."

In this view, the transatlantic alliance and its security commitment are more of a strategic liability for the United States than an asset. Seen from this perspective, it is extended deterrence rather than central (or essential) deterrence that has proved the most troublesome for the United States, both strategically and politically; its premises and consequences should therefore be reexamined. A central point in this line of argument is that extended deterrence requires a U.S. strategic posture that is fundamentally different and immensely riskier than would be required by central deterrence alone, primarily because extended deterrence entails a counterforce posture. This is so because in the absence of a protective umbrella over the United States only a counterforce strategy can limit damage and provide a measure of societal invulnerability for the U.S. population. Because extended deterrence implies that a U.S. president is willing to risk an attack on the United States, there must be sufficient protection for its people, as distinct from the protection of U.S. missiles, in order for such a deterrence posture to remain credible.

But a counterforce strategy is expensive and risky. It is expensive (and complicates arms control) because it requires a "hard target kill" capacity and therefore a large number of warheads and delivery systems. It is risky because it implies a preemptive first-strike strategy and undermines crisis stability by the insidious weapons-logic of "use them or lose them." In short: A counterforce strategy's main and perhaps only purpose can be its contribution to societal invulnerability. To obtain this invulnerability, the United States can develop defensive systems to obviate, neutralize, or at least complicate a Soviet attack; rely on a counterforce strategy; or renounce its commitment to extended deterrence.

This chain of reasoning inevitably leads to two conclusions, which tend to be reinforcing: (1) A defensive U.S. posture such as envisaged in the Reagan administration's Strategic Defense Initiative is necessary and/or (2) the more general political stance that, were it not for its commitment to come to the nuclear defense of an ally, the United States itself would not face a serious or fundamental security threat. Because a direct and initial attack on the United States by the Soviet Union is considered much less likely than the outbreak of conventional war in Europe and because the United States would retain a sufficient second-strike capability against Soviet value targets even after having suffered an attack, central or essential deterrence would—in this line of thinking—remain unimpaired. It is because of its alliance commitments that the United States runs unacceptable and basically implausible risks. Earl Ravenal summarizes this viewpoint.

> For this direct and essential *deterrent* purpose [i.e., one limited to the United States] social invulnerability is close to irrelevant; it is designed to protect, not to deter, and, by definition, the Soviets would already have attacked the United States (although they might have tried to limit their attack to a disarming strike against our nuclear forces). Certainly, in that circumstance, for direct and essential deterrence, the component of societal invulnerability that might be provided by our counterforce capability would be virtually useless; it would even be far less useful in limiting damage.

Rather, the case for our attainment of societal invulnerability concerns the validity of our guarantee to defend allies—that is, the efficacy of *extended deterrence*[6] (emphasis in original).

SDI: Strategic Disengagement and Independence

The idea of SDI, not to speak of its possible implementation, signifies the end of the transatlantic security alliance as we have known it. I say "signify" rather than "cause" because many factors have contributed to the devolution of the transatlantic security compact and because the consequences of the SDI program will run parallel to other historical developments, making it difficult to attribute to a single one the decisive impact. But I do believe that SDI, both as symbol and reality, stems from a profound reformulation of U.S. geopolitical orientation and therefore will have an equally profound effect on East-West relations, the nature of U.S.–West European diplomacy, and the bilateral U.S.-German connection.

Even before it has become a strategic reality, SDI has, as a political symbol, reshaped the diplomatic discourse between the United States and the Soviet Union and between the United States and its West European allies. It is in the nature of the transatlantic security relationship that symbols—strategic doctrines and sub-doctrines, contingency planning, diplomatic reassurances, nuclear control-sharing—are themselves a political reality, a condensed representation of diplomatic intentions, aimed at friend and foe alike. It is therefore not surprising that a program such as SDI, existing so far only as a technical blueprint, already reflects, in its intentions and consequences, a political program that exists here and now. The political effect precedes the strategic effect. Political costs have to be paid in advance, as it were, before the anticipated strategic benefits are realized in a distant future. For Europeans, and especially for Germans, the symbolic projection of U.S. strategic posture is at least as important as its technological structure. Although U.S. security planners often show a predilection toward the "hardware" aspects of the military balance, Europeans, perhaps because of historical experience, are less inclined to rely on the alleged certainties that come with numerical comparisons of force levels and more ready to entrust their national interests to the political balance of power.

The strategic ideas and political assumptions underlying the Reagan administration's SDI program are not totally new, a point to which I shall return presently. But in their compressed formulation, presented by the president in a highly dramatic fashion, these ideas do reverse long-standing precepts of U.S. strategy, impaired or even hollowed as these precepts may have become over the decades. Above all perhaps, the overarching paradigm of strategic deterrence, which had for decades served U.S. diplomacy in dealing with both opponents and allies, has been replaced by the paradigm of strategic defense. This itself has a subtle but profoundly disquieting effect on Western Europe, especially on the Federal Republic. For the contingency of defense, from the German perspective, has always implied the failure of deterrence. Deterrence is the operative strategic posture to prevent the outbreak of hostilities; defense is the operative posture once hostilities have in fact broken out, presumably involving the German people and German territory. Deterrence has come to signify, for the Germans, an anti-war or at least a pre-war military posture; defense is a war-time posture and signifies the ultimate calamity. Words—political metaphors, as it were— carry for the West Europeans (and the Soviets) a large meaning and portent.

There is another subtle but powerful aspect to the West European and West German response to SDI, and that is the ideological and political complexion of a U.S. administration that presents such a far-reaching program and announces such a deep reformulation of U.S. strategy. Europeans—Americans too, of course—place strategic thought in a political context. And here the Reagan administration had already in its first term created what one might call a reassurance gap, incurring with Western Europe a policy deficit both with respect to style and substance. The harsh cold war rhetoric, the patent disinterest in arms control, the macho celebrations of victory over a small island, the disarray on strategic matters within the administration itself—all these factors, and many more, handicapped this particular administration in articulating a drastic reversal of the postwar U.S. strategic posture. Perhaps no administration or president could have pulled this off successfully; but the Reagan administration, having aroused deep suspicions about its ultimate strategic intentions, appeared especially ill-suited for this task.

In many respects, the aspirations, frustrations, and political calculations that congealed in the Reagan administration's defense initiative were the culmination of long-standing issues in East-West relations and in the management of the Western alliance. SDI—or Star Wars, as it was soon dubbed—turned into a "super-issue" in which a number of sub-issues, important in their own right, became condensed in a critical mass of nuclear-strategic and political problems. In that respect, SDI does reflect a continuity of U.S. strategic concerns. In some ways, the debate occasioned by SDI is similar to the anti-ballistic missile debate of the late 1960s and early 1970s. Also, each U.S. president, beginning with Dwight D. Eisenhower, had considered (and rejected) the feasibility of replacing deterrence with defense; and each successive U.S. administration has, in some form or another, expressed uneasiness about a U.S. nuclear strategy that depends so much on the rationality of the opponent and that carries such a heavy risk for the U.S. population. More specifically, the principle of mutual assured destruction (MAD) had in certain ways become qualified by U.S. targeting doctrines, which concentrated more and more on Soviet nuclear forces rather than on Soviet cities; and there was a gradual evolution of U.S. strategy that combined the precepts of MAD and counterforce capacity. In turn, the general principle of mutual assured destruction became qualified by a principle of mutual assured invulnerability of second-strike, retaliatory forces.[7]

But the SDI idea is also different in some fundamental respects. New technologies exist or are presumed to come into being, the ABM Treaty would have to be modified or annulled to allow the legal deployment of missile defenses, and both sides are in the process of perfecting antisatellite systems. The most important difference, of course, lies in the changing strategic and political calculations that inform U.S. policy and in the central emphasis accorded strategic defense by the Reagan administration.

It is not easy to summarize the U.S. administration's rationale for SDI, in part because some of its intentions remain unarticulated, and in part because administration spokesmen "mis-spoke" on frequent occasions, correcting one another and offering differing interpretations of the feasibility, timing, technology-sharing, and strategic intentions of the SDI program. Some central points of the rationale, however, have emerged.

First, the policy of mutual assured destruction is said to be inadequate to prevent nuclear war. MAD, in essence the uncontested capacity of either side to retaliate in kind against a nuclear attack, provides only for uneasy stability and remains susceptible to irrational provocations, accidents, and conceivable attempts by third parties to trigger nuclear war between the two nuclear superpowers. This uneasy balance of terror became even less stable with the technological improvements of the 1970s, above all targeting accuracy, which offers the potential for preemption against U.S. hardened missile silos and other weapons facilities. U.S. retaliatory forces are becoming more and more vulnerable. Although the administration undertook an overdue modernization of U.S. offensive strategic forces, the survival of these forces could not be guaranteed and, even more importantly, successive U.S. governments would have even fewer options left to them in the future. The argument made by critics of SDI that even a dozen warheads leaking through the system would make it worthless is considered fallacious. To the contrary, "a system that allowed that level of leakage would make the ICBM worthless."[8]

Second, the mechanisms of arms control, as practiced over the decades, have failed to check the buildup of enormous stockpiles of nuclear weapons on both sides. In particular, when the ABM Treaty was signed in 1972 the technology to develop an SDI system did not exist, compelling the United States to choose the second-best option, mutual vulnerability, hoping for the subsequent reduction in offensive nuclear weapons through arms control. These expectations came to naught because of the obstructions of the Soviets, who, moreover, have in some instances transgressed the legal provisions of the ABM Treaty and have, in any case, launched an extensive research program for a strategic defense system of their own.

Third, SDI must concentrate, in the first instance, on defending against ICBMs because they are the most destabilizing elements in a nuclear arsenal and because the Soviet Union has invested 80 percent of its strategic budget in this type of weapon. This means, inter alia, that the Soviet Union is building a weapons arsenal that can have only one logical purpose: to launch or (equally important) threaten to launch a preemptive strike against U.S. retaliatory forces. The threat of a preemptive strike is therefore the most destabilizing factor in the arms race, causing it to spiral as each side proliferates its systems in order to retain a survivable retaliatory force.

Fourth, SDI is intended to protect populations, not weapons, to protect not just the United States but also its allies, and, at some future time, to protect even the Soviet Union if the appropriate mechanisms for technology sharing and drastic arms control measures can be fashioned. This is possible because the old-type ABM systems, with a terminal or point defense that could be easily overwhelmed with large numbers of warheads, can now be replaced with the SDI system, which attacks, in its boost phase, missiles rather than warheads. Because boost-phase defenses do not discriminate between the intended targets of ICBMs, be they in the United States, Europe, or Japan, U.S. allies are in effect covered under the same defensive umbrella. In particular, the Soviet SS-20, of concern to both Europe and Japan, is vulnerable to boost-phase destruction because of its high trajectory. For all these reasons and others, the boost-phase portion of SDI is a central and indispensable element in its strategic and political effectiveness. "Protecting weapons offers no real change in present policy. It simply strengthens the doctrine of mutual assured destruction. Protecting people, on the other hand, holds out the promise of dramatic change."[9]

Fifth, the various concerns voiced by Europeans are misplaced. It is indeed true that the deployment of SDI would mean a reemphasis on conventional forces in Europe, but new technology in the area of smart weapons would ease the way toward implementing that necessity, long overdue in any case. It is also true that Europeans need to be protected against shorter-range nuclear threats such as manned bombers or cruise missiles, but the anti-ICBM portion of SDI is only the first and central step and will be followed in time by additional steps that address many different kinds of threats. Those Europeans, like the French and British, who fear that a Soviet SDI system would reduce the importance of their independent nuclear forces, should feel reassured because "we're going to have an extended transition period as we shift from total reliance on offense to mixed offense-defense and eventually to heavy reliance on defense. That's going to take decades to occur, and throughout that time we'll obviously have to maintain a strong deterrent."[10]

The Problems of the Transition Period

The envisaged transition phase of the SDI program, however, in which a "mix" of offensive and defensive systems is anticipated, combines old and new NATO problems in a way that is especially problematic for the Federal Republic. The old NATO problem is of course the diminished credibility of the U.S. nuclear commitment to Europe. This problem will clearly remain during the transition phase of SDI because offensive systems continue to be the central element of the Western deterrence posture. To this is added a new NATO problem, created by the gradual establishment of SDI systems by both the United States and the Soviet Union. Were the two nuclear superpowers to escape gradually from their situation of mutual invulnerability, the threat of a U.S. first-use of nuclear weapons remains not only incredible but becomes also infeasible. The transition phase of SDI combines therefore the old problem of credibility with the new problem of feasibility. This immensely complicates NATO's strategy of pre-planned escalation (what West German planners call *vorbedachte Eskalation*), unraveling the carefully crafted and intricate web of NATO's contingency planning and targeting doctrines. A difficult period indeed.

In a sense, SDI seeks a return to the strategic situation of the 1950s. The massive retaliation doctrine of the Eisenhower years (which rested on the invulnerability of the United States and the vulnerability of the Soviet Union) and the NATO doctrine of flexible response (which ultimately rested on the principle of mutual vulnerability) are to be capped with a strategy that rests once again on U.S. invulnerability—but this time not because of the weakness of the opponent but because of the strength of U.S. defenses. Indeed, this view was expressed by Secretary of Defense Caspar W. Weinberger: "If we can get a system which is effective and which we know can render their weapons impotent, we could be back in a situation we were in, for example, when we were the only nation with a nuclear weapon."[11]

The reasoning of this statement can, if at all, apply only to U.S. central deterrence, not to extended deterrence. Even if a "Fortress America" can be created through an effective defensive umbrella (leaving aside the question of technological feasibility), it would be primarily central deterrence that would be strengthened, not extended deterrence—a state of affairs that British Foreign Minister Sir Geoffrey Howe criticized with the term "Maginot-Line" strategy. For the Western alliance there is a fundamental difference between U.S. invulnerability in the 1950s and the aimed-for invulnerability of the 1990s and the new century. Presumably the Soviet Union would be invulnerable as well, which would underline the possibility of U.S. nuclear decoupling from Europe and highlight in particular the precarious position of the Federal Republic. What the Germans call NATO's zones of "differentiated security," which have of course existed all along, would be made even more visible, raising the issue of whether a nuclear war might be limited to Europe.[12]

The question of whether the implementation of SDI would decouple or strengthen the U.S. connection to Western Europe cannot in any case be answered conclusively. The strategic-technological facts would allow, similar to the INF debate, totally opposite conclusions. Guesses about the range of possible decisions a U.S. president would consider in a crisis situation necessarily remain as speculative as do the convoluted scenarios of possible nuclear exchanges drawn up by strategic specialists. More easily assessed, because already visible, is the political decoupling effect the SDI program has created within the alliance. It has evoked in Europe responses that range from outright rejection (France), to partial assent (Great Britain) to hesitant endorsement (the Federal Republic). SDI follows closely on the heels of the INF debate, and the question arises whether NATO can accommodate this additional burden, at a time when the objectively different security interests of the United States and the Federal Republic have already created U.S.–West German frictions and when the SDI program has already caused a serious domestic rift in both countries. Indeed, both governments are divided within themselves: the U.S. government in trying to find a coherent articulation of the purposes of SDI; the West German government in trying to express its reservations in a way that does not burden U.S.–West German relations and the cohesion of the liberal-conservative coalition in Bonn. There is a clear danger that the security policies of the United States cause West Europeans to view U.S. policies more as a cause of East-West tensions than as a justifiable reaction to them. The new style of leadership in Moscow underlines that danger and leads to comparisons that are not always favorable to Washington.

In addition, the conventional capabilities of NATO will gain in importance, although in the short run the SDI idea tends to distract from the conventional force requirements of NATO, a development that General Bernard Rogers has already noted with concern. Both quantitative and qualitative improvements of NATO's conventional forces would become necessary, at heavy and perhaps prohibitive fiscal and political costs. Again, this is a burden that devolves primarily on the Federal Republic. Other NATO partners are unlikely to rely on the deterrent functions of conventional forces and to incur the costs connected with such an emphasis; geography, politics, and economics will stand in the way. France and Britain in particular are unlikely to agree to finance a larger conventional force, which means that an even more distinct division of labor will emerge betwen the nuclear West European powers and the conventional-force responsibilities of the Federal Republic. Should it prove impossible to persuade France to extend its own central deterrence to the Federal Republic, the ultimate taboo may be breached in 1995 when the nonproliferation treaty runs out: The Federal Republic may consider going nuclear.[13]

The Geopolitical Options of the Reagan Administration

Such reflections lead inevitably to the question of what political considerations underlie the SDI idea and what new arms control initiatives the second Reagan administration might be willing to entertain and negotiate. In an article in *Foreign Affairs,* Robert W. Tucker has suggested three ways in which, in principle, a faith in deterrence might be restored: (1) the restoration of U.S. strategic superiority; (2) U.S. withdrawal from "major postwar commitments," because it is *extended* deterrence that has lost its credibility and not the U.S. commitment to retaliate in response to a direct attack; and (3) the restoration of détente. As Tucker puts it:

> The effort to regain strategic superiority, or some semblance thereof, and a policy of withdrawal are two radically different ways to attempt a restoration of faith in deterrence. Either way may be pursued largely independent of the will and desire of the Soviet Union. This is one of their undoubted attractions and is to be sharply contrasted with the third course, détente, which is evidently dependent on the cooperation of the Soviet government. The attraction of détente, on the other hand, is that it is easier to pursue than strategic superiority while less likely to result in the sacrifice that withdrawal probably entails.[14]

Clearly, each of those three options not only carries with it distinct implications for the present and future arms control policies of the United States but also raises fundamental questions about the geopolitical stance of the Reagan administration. Pursuing the first two options would, in different ways, raise serious and perhaps debilitating obstacles to the future of East-West arms control, whereas the third would appear to hold the most promise. Looking at the record of the Reagan administration, it appears that, in the absence of pursuing détente, Washington has pursued the alternatives of strategic superiority and, with modification, of withdrawal.

It is in this context that SDI obtains its central geopolitical significance. In my estimation, the basic purpose of the SDI program is twofold. It is designed to advance, in conjunction, those two U.S. geopolitical options for restoring faith in deterrence that Robert Tucker saw as "radically different": the restoration of U.S. strategic superiority and U.S. withdrawal from the obligations of extended deterrence. I believe that the Reagan administration is pursuing both options simultaneously. These options may be analytically different, but they have, in this administration, coalesced into complementary compulsions, fed by powerful resentments toward the Soviet Union and by equally powerful frustrations with U.S. allies. They evoke a deep historical resonance as well. For what could have a larger appeal to the U.S. population and many of their leaders than a geopolitical strategy that permits the United States to be safe as well as independent, superior in competing with the adversary in the only area in which the adversary can claim superpower status, and liberated from the complications and risks of managing entangling alliances? The U.S. hopes associated with SDI incorporate and accommodate both compulsions in equal measure, making them mutually supportive in their strategic, political, and emotional logic.[15]

But if I am correct in my assessment, then the intentions reflected in SDI not only reverse the long-standing principle of strategic deterrence but also eviscerate the principle of political containment. For if containment has meant anything in the postwar diplomacy of the United States, it has meant and required a deep and continuing U.S. engagement in the affairs of Europe. The political calculations that had all along informed the strategy of containment—that the division of the Continent stabilized the European and global balance of power and hence was in the U.S. interest—have not lost their plausibility in the 1980s even though their implementation has become immensely more difficult. It is, or in any case should be, a fundamental U.S. national interest to remain centrally involved in the present and future European political order. On the military-strategic level, however, a contradictory but equally plausible set of calculations has begun to inform U.S. strategic thinking—namely, that the U.S. nuclear commitment to Western Europe might be more of a liability than an asset, and that U.S. interests require a more detached and qualified association with Europe, perhaps even disengagement. Political imperatives, suggesting continuing engagement, are in conflict with military-strategic imperatives, suggesting disengagement. Political proximity and strategic distance—how are they to be reconciled? The answer to that question will determine the future shape of the European political order and the Federal Republic's emplacement in it.

Notes

1. For a fuller discussion of this connection, see Wolfram F. Hanrieder, *Fragmente der Macht: Die Aussenpolitik der Bundesrepublik* (Munich: Piper, 1981) and "Arms Control and the Federal Republic," in Wolfram F. Hanrieder, ed., *Technology, Strategy, and Arms Control* (Boulder, Colo.: Westview Press, 1985), pp. 49-64.

2. George W. Ball, "White House Roulette," *New York Review of Books*, November 8, 1984, p. 6.

3. See Michael Howard, "Reassurance and Deterrence: Western Defense in the 1980s," *Foreign Affairs*, vol. 61, no. 2 (Winter 1982-1983), pp. 309-324.

4. Cf. Strobe Talbott, *Deadly Gambits* (New York: Alfred A. Knopf, 1984).

5. See McGeorge Bundy, George F. Kennan, Robert S. McNamara, and Gerard Smith, "Nuclear Weapons and the Atlantic Alliance," *Foreign Affairs*, vol. 60, no. 4 (Spring 1982), pp. 753-768. For a German response to Bundy et al., see Karl Kaiser, Georg Leber, Alois Mertes, and Franz-Joseph Schulze, "Nuclear Weapons and the Preservation of Peace," *Foreign Affairs*, vol. 60, no. 5 (Summer 1982), pp. 1157-1170.

6. Earl C. Ravenal, *Nato: The Tides of Discontent*. Policy Papers in International Affairs no. 23 (Berkeley, Calif.: Institute of International Studies, 1985), pp. 23-24.

7. See Desmond Ball, "Targeting for Strategic Deterrence," Adelphi Papers no. 185 (London: The International Institute for Strategic Studies, Summer 1983) and M. Leitenberg, "Announced Changes in United States Nuclear Weapon Targeting Policy" (Stockholm: The Swedish Institute of International Affairs, September/October 1980).

8. George A. Keyworth II, *Security and Stability: The Role for Strategic Defense*. Policy Paper no. 1 (San Diego, Calif.: University of California Institute on Global Conflict and Cooperation, May 1985), p. 8.

9. Ibid., p. 7.

10. Ibid., p. 8. For some well-reasoned German responses, see Claus Richter, "Strategische Verteidigungsinitiative (SDI): Kriegsführung oder Kriegsverhinderung?" in *Aus Politik und Zeitgeschichte*, B-14-15/85, pp. 15-33. Col. Richter, attached to Supreme Headquarters, Allied Powers, Europe, is especially skeptical with respect to the possibility of providing defenses against short- and medium-range nuclear munitions in Europe. See also the lengthy study by Wolfgang Schreiber, *Die Strategische Verteidigungsinitiative: Vorgeschichte, Konzeption, Perspektiven* (Melle: Verlag Ernst Knoth, 1985), undertaken by the Konrad Adenauer Foundation. This study is especially interesting because it takes a rather positive if guarded view of SDI. The argument concluding this study practically accepts

as a given the nuclear decoupling of the United States from Western Europe. What makes this, to me, especially astonishing is that his conclusion is not fundamentally different from the premises of the "von Bulow paper," which raised such a fuss in Germany earlier in the year.

11. Cited in George W. Ball, "The War for Star Wars," *New York Reivew of Books,* April 11, 1985, p. 40.

12. When President Reagan was asked if he thought an exchange of nuclear weapons in Europe between the United States and the Soviet Union could be limited or if escalation was inevitable, he replied: "I could see where you could have the exchange of tactical weapons in the field without it bringing either one of the major powers to pushing the button." *Washington Post,* November 1, 1981.

13. Cf. David Garnham, "Extending Deterrence with German Nuclear Weapons," *International Security,* vol. 11, no. 1 (Summer 1985), pp. 96–110.

14. Robert W. Tucker, "The Nuclear Debate," *Foreign Affairs,* vol. 63, no. 1 (Fall 1984), p. 31.

15. This line of thinking is especially pronounced with Americans who urge a more Pacific-oriented U.S. diplomacy, an attitude that is deeply rooted in the present administration as well as in some segments of the Republican party. Cf. Eberhard Rein, "Die pazifische Herausforderung—Gefahren und Chancen fur Europa," *Europa-Archiv* 39, Heft 4 (1984), pp. 101–110; Wolfram F. Hanrieder, "Grundprobleme der deutsch-amerikanischen Beziehungen," *Merkur,* 37, Heft 5 (July 1983), pp. 518–530. The fundamental differences in the Atlantic or Pacific orientations of U.S. diplomacy, and their domestic sources, were, in the late 1930s, analyzed by Charles and Mary Beard, who labeled them "collective internationalism" and "imperial isolationism" (*America in Midpassage* [New York: Macmillan, 1939]).

Acronyms

ABM	anti-ballistic missile
ASAT	anti-satellite weapon
ATBM	anti-tactical ballistic missile
BMD	ballistic missile defense
CDE	East-West Conference on Disarmament in Europe
CDU	Christian Democratic Union (FRG)
CSCE	Conference on Security and Cooperation in Europe
CSU	Christian Social Union (FRG)
EC	European Community
EDI	European Defense Initiative
EORSAT	electronic ocean reconnaissance satellite
FDP	Free Democratic Party (FRG)
FRG	Federal Republic of Germany
GDR	German Democratic Republic
GLCM	ground-launched cruise missile
ICBM	intercontinental ballistic missile
INF	intermediate-range nuclear force
LRTNF	long-range theater nuclear force
MAD	mutual assured destruction
MBFR	mutual and balanced force reduction
MIRV	multiple, independently targeted reentry vehicle
MLF	multilateral force
NATO	North Atlantic Treaty Organization
OTA	Office of Technology Assessment
PII	Pershing II missile
R&D	research and development
RORSAT	radar ocean reconnaissance satellite
RV	reentry vehicle
SALT	Strategic Arms Limitation Talks
SDI	Strategic Defense Initiative
SED	Socialist Unity Party (GDR)
SLBM	submarine-launched ballistic missile
SPD	Social Democratic Party (FRG)
SSBN	ballistic missile nuclear submarine
START	Strategic Arms Reduction Talks
WP	Warsaw Pact

About the Editor and Contributors

Wolfram F. Hanrieder is professor of political science at the University of California, Santa Barbara, and chairman of the Advisory Committee, Program on Global Peace and Security. He has written numerous books and articles on the transatlantic alliance, West German and West European foreign policies, and national security policy and arms control.

Jonathan Dean, now arms control adviser of the Union of Concerned Scientists, was U.S. representative to the NATO–Warsaw Pact Force Reduction Negotiations in Vienna (the MBFR talks) between 1978 and 1981, having served as deputy U.S. representative since the beginning of those talks in 1973. He was deputy U.S. negotiator in the 1971 Four Power Berlin Agreement with the Soviet Union.

Sidney D. Drell is professor, deputy director, and executive head of theoretical physics at the Stanford Linear Accelerator Center, Stanford University, and codirector of the Stanford Center for International Security and Arms Control. He has been a member of the president's Science Advisory Committee and a consultant for the National Security Council and the U.S. Arms Control and Disarmament Agency. He has published numerous papers in theoretical physics and several books, including *Facing the Threat of Nuclear Weapons* (1983).

John P. Holdren is professor of energy and resources at the University of California, Berkeley; chairman of the Federation of American Scientists; and a member of the Executive Committee of the Pugwash Conferences on Science and World Affairs.

Sanford Lakoff is professor of political science at the University of California, San Diego, where he served as founding chairman of the department from 1975–1979. He has written in the areas of the history of political thought and the relations of science and government. His publications include *Equality in Political Philosophy* (1964), *Science and the Nation* (co-author, 1962), and *Energy and American Values* (co-author, 1982).

Eckhard Lübkemeier is an analyst with the Friedrich-Ebert-Stiftung and has published extensively in the area of security issues.

Peter H. Merkl is professor of political science at the University of California, Santa Barbara. He is the author of *German Foreign Policies, West and East* (1974) and the editor of *West German Foreign Policy: Dilemmas and Directions* (Chicago Council of Foreign Relations, 1983) and *Political Violence and Terror: Motifs and Motivations* (1986).

Dietrich Stobbe is a leader of the SPD and a member of the foreign relations committee of the Bundestag. He was formerly governing mayor of Berlin and resident director of the Friedrich-Ebert-Stiftung in New York (1981–1983).

Paul E. Zinner is professor of political science at the University of California, Davis. His most recent book is *East-West Relations in Europe: Observations and Advice from the Sidelines, 1971–1982.*